Mills College Library
from

Edwin P. Cunningham

Boston
February
195|3

NINETEENTH CENTURY
ENGLISH
POTTERY AND PORCELAIN

The Faber Monographs on Pottery and Porcelain

Edited by W. B. HONEY

★

★

OTHER TITLES TO FOLLOW

A. EARTHENWARE JUG. STAFFORDSHIRE
EARLY NINETEENTH CENTURY
HEIGHT, $5\frac{3}{4}$ IN.
See page 14

NINETEENTH CENTURY
ENGLISH
POTTERY AND PORCELAIN

by

GEOFFREY BEMROSE

FABER AND FABER

24 Russell Square
London

First published in mcmlii
by Faber and Faber Limited
24 Russell Square London W.C. 1
Printed in Great Britain by
R. MacLehose and Company Limited
The University Press Glasgow
Blocks made and colour plates printed by
Fine Art Engravers Limited, Esher

To
THE POTTERS of STOKE ON TRENT

'We make our pots of what we potters are'

ACKNOWLEDGEMENT

Acknowledgement is made to all those who have lent specimens for illustration. Where no reference is made on the plate the specimen has been lent by the City Museum and Art Gallery, Stoke-on-Trent, to whom special thanks are due.

FOREWORD

The nineteenth century was an age of great confusion of values in the arts, and the ceramic art suffered no less than others from misdirected effort and mistaken enthusiasms. While the early part of the century largely lived, so to speak, on the accumulated artistic capital of the preceding period, the latter part was chiefly occupied with the deliberate revival of former styles. In neither phase can it be said that any new or truly original style was created.

Yet in spite of unfavourable conditions the native genius of the English potters did succeed in producing wares which are both beautiful and of permanent value; and it is a task worth while to discover them in the welter of *parvenu* vulgarity that marked the period after the Napoleonic Wars, and in the monstrous outgrowth of 'applied art' of the years that led up to and followed the Great Exhibition. Even in the museum-taught academic revivals of the last part of the century, some good work was done.

To distinguish the movements that produced this vital work has been Mr. Bemrose's difficult but not ungrateful task. He passes in review the admirably simple 'cottage china' and lustre ware of the New Hall type and its kindred earthenware, as well as the Worcester, Derby, Spode, Nantgarw and Swansea, Coalport and other porcelains which were its opulent contemporaries and successors. The charming blue-printed ware, and the entirely English brown stonewares of the Midlands and Lambeth are among the earlier wares described and illustrated. Many pretty Victorian fancies also find a place here beside the productions of the Revived Rococo, Gothic and Renaissance styles, before the revival of handicraft makes its appearance, with de Morgan and the Martin brothers, heralding the studio pottery of the present day.

The scope of the book has not allowed a detailed historical treatment, with marks and dates for all the factories. Nor is the time ripe for such a work. What is needed is a discriminating perspective view, and this Mr. Bemrose has admirably provided.

W. B. H.

CONTENTS

CONTENTS

ILLUSTRATIONS

COLOUR PLATES

MONOCHROME PLATES
after page 58

INTRODUCTION

Fifty years have passed since the close of the nineteenth century but we are still without a clear view of the minor arts of England during that much-maligned period. That they are dull and uninviting is generally agreed but, even so, they deserve more sympathetic consideration than has hitherto been their lot. The few available accounts of the pottery of the period are either tantalisingly short chapters in the art histories, or compilations from trade and exhibition catalogues making no pretence of critical judgment.

The reasons for this neglect are well known. On the one hand we may agree with a celebrated critic when he asserts that 'what the Victorians made and called art was almost always rubbish' and that 'Victorian taste was almost wholly vile'. Or it may be felt that we have indulged too long that disrespect which is apt to be the attitude of the modern towards the not-so-modern. One of the difficulties in appraising the arts of a recent period is this impatience with the works of our elders, salutary though it may be. Over-generous enthusiasm such as our great-grandfathers accorded the arts and manufactures of their day, is bound to lead to a reversal of feeling in the succeeding generations and it is only with the passage of time that a true perspective can be found.

It seems, therefore, that the time is appropriate to consider the pottery of nineteenth-century England in an endeavour to discover some of the virtues peculiar to that age. Our concern will range from magnificent garnitures for the salon to humble ornaments for the cottage chimney-piece. Between these extremes we shall observe a host of pots technically as good as they are, for the greater part, aesthetically negligible. Some of this pottery can be said to have acquired a period flavour which may be found 'amusing' but of personal style it has none. Nor could it expect to have. Devoted to the imitation of the arts of almost every age and country it could scarcely hope to achieve a style of its own. Yet, in a sense, the Victorians did impart a feeling to much of the pottery after 1830 that is quite unlike anything else. From the multitude of styles and influences there emerges a recognisable quality, at once solid and sentimental, that belongs only to that period; although not strictly accurate, we know it as 'Victorian'.

1

In the following selection of one hundred and seventy examples, an attempt is made to show some of the characteristic English wares of the century.

Much can be learned of a people by the pottery that they have left behind them. In pre-literary ages we are almost dependent on the ceramic record as the archaeologist has so often demonstrated. Even in recent times we can form a vivid picture of a people from a study of their pottery. For example, the lack of joyousness implicit in the Puritan outlook is clearly shown by the lugubrious pottery of Cromwell's austere regime. Similarly, the gaiety of Restoration England is evident in all the arts of the day, not least in the contemporary 'delft' pottery. But a century of quick-moving change such as that bounded by the years 1800–1900 is not so readily understood.

The continued evolution from agriculture to mechanised industry between 1800–1850 had a profound effect on the manners of England. Fashion, which had persisted for twenty or thirty years in the spacious Georgian days, now lasted for ten years at most. The desire for novelty which appears to be a feature of town life, arose in the 1820's; a consciousness of the greater world became evident as the century advanced. The greatly increased density of population, particularly in the Midlands and the North, brought an altered tempo of life which is well illustrated by the pottery of the period. Clearly, any consideration of nineteenth century pottery and porcelain will need sub-division and the following by no means ideal classification is suggested for the sake of clarity.

Porcelain being more susceptible to fashion is more readily classified than earthenware. Between 1800 and 1830 much of the porcelain was an English version of current French styles or a re-hash of the more successful productions of eighteenth-century Worcester, Derby and Chelsea. From 1830 to 1845 a kind of English rococo was in vogue and was followed by the multifarious wares produced for the Great Exhibition of 1851 which defy classification. Oddly enough, the 'Gothick' trend of the Exhibition as a whole was not evident in the porcelain displays. By 1875 or shortly afterwards the teachings of William Morris began to influence ceramic design and the porcelain of the period exhibits the first really original designs of the century. The minor influences also were from sources outside the industry. Apart from the immigrant French artists introduced by Mintons and the Cauldon factory, designs were commissioned from well-known painters. Alfred Stevens, Sir Charles Robinson, Walter Crane and even Stacey Marks designed for pottery. The influence of Government schools of design began to have effect and artists who were at the schools in the late 50's were now in a position to design for the important factories.

INTRODUCTION

Last of all came the 'Nineties' which, though often concerned with *art nouveau* and other *fin de siècle* absurdities, ushered in the modern period.

Earthenware was not so greatly affected by fashion though the finer wares emulated porcelain styles whenever possible. Apart from peasant wares, which require separate consideration, the story of nineteenth century English earthenware is that of a steady expansion of a relatively few basic shapes and patterns and the continued development of technique. This led to an ever increasing concern for the requirements of mass production and many important technical discoveries were made. Improvements in production methods encouraged the subdivision of the industry. Thus, bone-china became an independent section of ceramics and was located at Longton in North Staffordshire. The same process occurred in the manufacture of refractories and heavy clay products, sanitary wares, tiles, domestic earthenware and electrical wares which became concentrated in an area or, quite often, in a single factory.

For our purpose it will be found convenient to consider first the period 1800–1850. To label it 'Early Industrial' may serve, though this is not strictly accurate, as a measure of industrialisation had been achieved by 1780. Much of the pottery and porcelain of the early nineteenth century was, in fact, no more than a vulgarian edition of the products of 1780–1800. Our concern however, is with the new ideas of the new century and we observe, perhaps for the first time in our history, what has come to be known as class catering. Previous to 1800 one, or perhaps two kinds of domestic pottery, with slight variation, had served to meet all needs. By 1830 it was evident that the middle classes and the 'lower orders' also had to be considered. Three main types were evolved to meet the needs of the community. Firstly, there was the sumptuous porcelain for the wealthy classes produced at Derby and Worcester and by Spode, Davenport and others. Secondly, the less ornate but by no means cheap porcelain of Wales and Rockingham and the fine earthenwares and 'stone chinas' of Staffordshire made for middle class folk; and lastly the common earthenware and cottage china for the poorer people. To attempt a summary of the porcelain and earthenware of the century would be hazardous but the following broad divisions are suggested: (*a*) 1800–1830—an overspill of the previous century declining towards the end of the period but including many new processes, i.e. underglaze transfer printing; perhaps the earliest Parian experiments; class catering; increased mass production. (*b*) 1840–70—The Great Exhibitions. (*c*) 1870–85—The influence of schools of design and museums; William Morris. (*d*) 1885–1900—*Art nouveau*; studio potters. The rural population, especially in the south-

3

ern half of England, was content with the products of the nearby country pottery for most needs. Only the tea service, invariably an article of decoration, was obtained from farther afield.

We begin our survey with these dateless country wares which will set the stage and provide a basis for comparison.

COUNTRY POTTERIES

In the everyday utensils of life, English craftsmen have generally been as good as and often better than their continental brethren and the need to make a new vessel for a new use has never found them wanting, neither in good sense, nor simple dignity. It may be that the invention has borrowed from the past but it has invariably shown a keen grasp of those twin essentials—comeliness and utility. This plain sobriety is perhaps our truest national characteristic in the minor arts and is best seen in the work of men unaware of fashionable models. Much of it, in fact, is purely intuitive. Some of our best pottery has found expression in simple objects; design, if somewhat pedestrian, has seldom lacked sincerity. It is when we have ventured into extravaganza that we have become ridiculous. There is no English baroque pottery, but the nineteenth century provides some romantic essays in rococo which are best forgotten. As a people, we lack that sense of regardlessness which is so necessary in an approach to plastic art and this is especially true of the pottery of nineteenth century England.

Country potteries had arisen in many parts of England during mediaeval times. Most of them were of short life but some persisted until well into modern times. A few appear to have been worked by itinerant potters—gypsies to the villagers—others were in the hands of a local family for a century or even longer. In the North these simple potworks were known as sun-kilns from the sun-pan, a salient feature which was common to them all. This consisted of a stone-lined pit sunk in the ground in which the clay was matured by solar action. Traces of these sun-kilns are often found, and at a site recently discovered at Ipstones near Leek it was possible to form a fair idea of the layout of the works. The site had been chosen near to a stream on the boulder clay with outcropping coal near at hand. Lead ore was dug in a field a short distance away and coarse white sand, almost pure silica, was obtained by the stream. All the requisite basic materials of the potter, therefore, were available in a small area. A rectangular tank lined with slabs of millstone grit was provided with a division where the clay could be 'blunged' or mixed with water and brought to a creamy consistency. This liquid was then sieved into a sun-pan where evaporation took place. The buildings were evidently of the simplest description, doubtless mere thatched hovels. The oven, a simple hob-mouthed type, was clearly to be seen after the pottery wasters had been cleared away. These broken pots were of one type formed from a red firing clay, coated with a lead glaze coloured with manganese. Bold pitchers, vinegar kegs, mugs, bowls, bottles and settling pans of simple but majestic form appear to have been the stock-in-trade, as one would expect from a pottery supplying the needs of an agricultural district. Similar pot hovels existed in the early nineteenth century at Hanley and Goldenhill in Staffordshire and at places as far apart as East Anglia and the Welsh marches. Apparently after supplying the needs of a district for a few years the potters moved on after the manner of the mediaeval tile-makers. It is likely that the restless nature of many pottery workers in early industrial days may have been due to wandering habits formed in youth whilst employed in country potteries. Occasionally these gypsy potters settled in a district as, for example, the Hallidays, who were at Howcans near Halifax for over a century and the Catheralls who worked the Swilling Hill, Denholme and Bradshaw Head potworks also in Yorkshire. In the richer agricultural districts of Southern England the rustic potteries enjoyed a more stable patronage and were able to continue in one area for a long period employing, as the occasion offered, simple mechanical aids. It is convenient therefore to refer these permanent potteries to their counties and we can speak of the peasant wares of Kent, Sussex, North Devon and Somerset. Smaller village pottery works became associated with Blackburton in Lancashire, Fareham in Hampshire, Verwood in Dorset, Truro in Cornwall, and at many other places in Yorkshire, Derbyshire and South Wales. Leadglazed red or buff clay wares, usually with well marked local characteristics were produced.

THE KENTISH POTTERIES at Pembury, Brabourne, High Halden (1), Deal, Sevenoaks and Dunkirk, to mention the more prominent, made crude but not unpleasing rustic wares during the century. Clay from the Wealden which fires to a deep red, and alluvial clays from the Deal area, of a light pink colour, were used, often with crude slip decoration. In some of the productions it is possible to discern a faint flavour of Wrotham slipware which was famous in the seventeenth to eighteenth centuries and it is likely that a continuity may have existed.

THE POTTERY OF SUSSEX forms a more coherent class, marked by sound workmanship in a limited field. The Brede pot works appears to be earliest in date for a pottery existed at Broadland Wood in the fifteenth century (2). Burgess Hill specialized in 'agate' wares and goblets, posset pots and basins appear to have been favourite produc-

---

(1) *Plate* 5A; (2) *Plate* 5B.

tions. At Rye and Brede, bold jars and pipkins were made with impressed decoration—often sprays of leaves—and garnished with inscriptions from printers' type which were filled with slip (1). This feature which is found on the smaller wares of Bethersden and Dicker is peculiar to Sussex. The streaked glaze, a simple but charming effect due to the presence of iron in the clay, is found on most Sussex wares. Small pot works are known to have existed at Uckfield (2), Hellingley, East Grinstead and Hastings. Domestic pottery for the country cottage and farm constitute the bulk of the Sussex wares; such things as tea jars, milk churns, flasks in the form of pocket watches and barrel flasks are common.

Rustic pottery is of considerable antiquity in NORTH DEVON where the splendid jugs of Barnstaple are thought to have been made as early as the thirteenth century. The town is still concerned in the manufacture of pottery but at other places in North Devon a vigorous craft has been allowed to die out. Bideford appears to have closed in 1896 and at Fremington, where three or four generations of the Fishley family potted, nothing now remains (3). Michael Cardew, the studio potter, and at least two well-known Staffordshire pottery manufacturers received their early training at Fremington. The Bideford pottery was famous for its fine harvest jugs decorated in sgraffito by Henry Phillips who died in 1894.

THE SOMERSET WARES, which are quite distinctive, were made at Donyatt and Crock Street near Ilminster. Fuddling cups with intertwined handles bear late seventeenth century dates but most of the surviving jugs belong to the late eighteenth to early nineteenth century. Incised decoration is the rule and the glaze is usually tinged with copper green. Space will not permit an extended study of our rustic wares but mention must be made of the slip ware of Buckley in Flintshire and the admirable barm pots or salt kits made at the Weatheriggs Pottery at PENRITH (4). Country slip ware is companionable stuff and serves to remind us in these days of mechanical sophistication of the time when the potter was master of the craft in all its aspects. Less usefully these wares provide a model for much of the craft-ware sold in the art shops. The best country wares were made by men who recognised, perhaps instinctively, what has been exalted in these latter days into a cult. Truth to material and aptness for purpose are not at all new and it is instructive to observe how many of the requirements of daily life were served by these humble potters. Pilchard pots, harvest jugs, ovens, lamb feeders and even 'bawd pans' were made in the Devon potteries. Spice chests, money boxes, puzzle jugs, mugs,

---

(1) *Plates* 2A, B; (2) *Plate* 5B; (3) *Plates* 3A, 5B; (4) *Plate* 4.

cradles and bird calls were made in Yorkshire. The Sussex wares have been mentioned, but yeast tiles, candlesticks and gaily decorated taws for the once popular game of carpet bowls were made everywhere. To-day our artist potters look to the pottery of China but the simple good form and appropriate decoration of many an English country jug or bowl may still contribute to the conception of our English pottery aesthetic.

Although not strictly in the same category as country pot-works, a number of small factories in Great Britain were producing humble wares which were sold in the cheapest markets during the century. The stoneware potteries of the Greater London area which trace their descent from Dwight of Fulham continued to make brown salt glazed pottery which is often indistinguishable from the wares of the seventeenth century (1). The fine white stonewares of Turner and his school were imitated in BROWN STONEWARE by Kishere of Mortlake (2). Pistol flasks were a speciality of Stephen Green of Lambeth and other factories making brown stonewares were located at Lambeth and at Vauxhall where the large works of James Stiff produced many kinds of commercial and decorative stoneware. Brown stoneware potteries existed at Nottingham, Bristol, the Waverley Pottery Portobello, Glasgow and elsewhere. Some of the best wares were from a group of small pot works in Derbyshire where an ancient tradition of brown stoneware centres upon Crich and dates back to 1700. Mantelpiece ornaments of animals made at Chesterfield (3) are a pleasant and decorative use of stoneware. Spirit flasks made at Denby and elsewhere about the time of the Reform Bill of 1832 bear caricatures of politicians of the time. The unfortunate William Coffee who had been a kilnman at the Coade factory at Lambeth was living at Derby in 1810 and it is likely that he modelled for the Derbyshire stoneware factories at Brampton (4), Codnor Park, Hartshorne and Derby town. This brown stoneware strain persisted throughout the century and culminated in the consciously artistic wares of Doulton of Lambeth (5) and the pottery of the brothers Martin of Southall (6).

---

(1) *Plates* 6B, c; (2) *Plate* 6A; (3) *Plate* 7A; (4) 7B; (5) *Plates* 88, 92A, c, 93B; (6) *Plates* 89, 90, 91.

2

PEASANT EARTHENWARES

Even the larger factories did not disdain the ever-growing working-class market and from 1810 onwards a class of boldly painted earthen wares, invariably in bright enamel colours was produced in North Staffordshire, Wales, Yorkshire and Scotland. A cream coloured earthenware made by Ring of Bristol and decorated by William Fifield junior from 1820 to 1850 is somewhat similar in feeling but more accomplished. The firms of Adams of Greenfields, Tunstall (1), Rogers of Burslem, Davenport of Longport (2) and the Copeland factory, are known to have made the simpler 'peasant' type of ware. The decoration was by artists accustomed to work in resist for lustre wares, an indication not only of the readiness of decorators to turn from one class of ware to another but also of the many different types produced by a single factory in a relatively short space of time. Pottery pattern books of the period are indeed weighty tomes and give added proof of the enterprise and multiplicity of the undertakings of the average nineteenth century factory. The versatility of a factory employing less than 250 hands was amazing; fine bone china, fine stoneware, 'ironstone china', transfer printed, lustred and enamelled earthenwares and figures were current productions. Excellent mugs and bowls banded in bright colours were made at Prestonpans, the Yorkshire potteries, Burton-on-Trent and, of course, at the Staffordshire potteries. The bowls had a long life and were an important article of export to West Africa where the natives used them as food vessels until comparatively recent times. A belated use of slip—the potter's term for clay watered to a creamy consistency—made its appearance early in the century usually for the decoration of jugs, ale mugs and other domestic utensils. By its very nature, slip requires to be trailed or drawn-on to the pottery and in the late seventeenth and early eighteenth century some magnificent trailed slipware was produced by Toft, Simpson and others. The nineteenth century potter used slip in various ways, two of which were new—firstly by combining two bands of contrasting colour into a motif (3) and secondly, by trailing

(1) *Plate* 12; (2) *Plate* 13B; (3) *Plate* 26B.

two colours side by side and then working them together either by a brush or the finger (1). Slip banding also appears on nineteenth century wares (2). It is often asserted that the Industrial Revolution destroyed all folk art in England. It did not. Staffordshire potters were quite capable of frolicking with Continental porcelain and, at the same time, retaining a peculiarly indigenous English style for the humbler markets.

'MOCHA' WARE. Early in the century a simple but quite original class of pottery which has considerable peasant charm originated in North Staffordshire—it is said at the Adams factories at Cobridge and Tunstall. Known as 'Mocha' ware from the decoration which bore a striking resemblance to the ornamental quartz called Mocha-stone, it rapidly became popular in taverns and in cottage homes. The best and earliest pieces were on a creamware body (3) but cheap white earthenware and a hard cane body were used later. The method was as follows:— upon the leather-hard clay, a ground colour was laid, usually grey, blue, or yellow upon which pigment was introduced and allowed to run. This pigment was usually brown in colour and was mixed with a brew of tobacco and hop which controlled the pattern. The result was a fascinating dendritic effect variously likened to trees, feathers or moss. A chestnut-brown ground is found on the early creamware specimens; various shades of brown, straw, orange or green are not infrequent on early pieces but white is rare. The moss-like decoration was commonly brown, but green, blue and black specimens are known; pink is found only on modern pieces *circa* 1880 and later. The market for which the ware was intended is shown by the shapes. Ale mugs, jugs, ale-tasters, chamber-pots, shrimp and nut measures and pitchers are common. Articles for the dinner-table—sugar bowls, honey pots, butter pots, salts, pepper and mustard pots, teapots, coffee pots and basins are less frequent. Although essentially a utilitarian ware Mocha was sometimes used as a decoration for ornamental pieces such as flower vases and pot-pourri bowls with real ceramic distinction. These pieces invariably show refinement of potting. The known makers are Adams of Tunstall, Cork and Edge of Burslem, Broadhurst of Fenton, Tams of Longton, MacIntyre of Cobridge, Pinder and Bourne of Burslem, Green of Church Gresley, Maling of Newcastle-on-Tyne and factories in the Stockton area, Clydeside and perhaps at Swansea and Sunderland. Even Creil in France, a factory staffed at this time by Staffordshire workmen, used Mocha effects on a porcelain body. One unidentified factory, perhaps Glasgow, produced some admirable pitchers with Mocha decoration in the form of thistle sprays on a caneware

---

(1) *Plate* 27; (2) *Plates* 26A, B, 27; (3) *Plate* 26A.

body. Incidentally Mocha ware provides a fascinating study of Excise stamps as the ale mugs and beer jugs are usually marked with measure of capacity in various ways, either on applied lead plugs or bands, but sometimes as prints or moulds on the vessel. The most common method of marking was by the sand blast stencil and the cyphers G.R., W.R., and V.R. are not uncommon.

EARTHENWARES

By 1800 a large number of earthenware bodies were being made in England. The improved creamware of Josiah Wedgwood was still important but many new bodies had been introduced in the closing years of the eighteenth century, some of which were intended for special purposes. Others, frankly invented to undercut prices, were of poor quality and deserve no mention in the account which follows. The so-called 'dry bodies' continued in use; the black basaltes of Wedgwood were decorated in enamel colours at Etruria but the red body which had been in use since the time of Dwight and Elers now underwent considerable development in the hands of tea-pot manufacturers. In both glazed and unglazed states the red body became an important article of commerce and though confined to humble kitchen wares, some pleasing shapes were produced. Special pottery bodies were used for transfer printed wares and for lustre. Caneware was much used and a hard chalky body containing clays, stone, lime and flint was used for dinner wares and occasionally for figures. The pearl body was made by many factories engaged in better-class productions as was a drab body which was effectively decorated in applied relief after the manner of jasper. Both were admirable. Most of these new materials were known before 1800, it must be admitted, but ceaseless rule of thumb experiments at the bench and in the slip-house brought them to a high state of perfection. By 1830 the variety of pottery and porcelain bodies was bewildering and no attempt can be made to enumerate even a tithe of them. Instead, an attempt will be made to indicate the more important types of pottery that may be claimed as typical of the nineteenth century.

Good earthenwares continued to be made at Leeds by Hartley Greens & Co. until 1820 and from then until 1840 by Wainwright & Co. Some of the wares were obviously eighteenth century reproductions, an activity that persisted until late in the century as many collectors know to their cost, but some new issues were well potted and turned on the lathe (1).

More original work came from the Staffordshire potteries at this

(1) *Plate* 15 and 16a.

time and the painting in sepia on a salmon pink ground as practised at the Davenport works is delightful (1). Even the smaller factories were capable of such charming pottery as the dish (2) and the jug (3).

These are but minor products, however, and we pass on to the important and typically 'Victorian' earthenwares of the first half of the century. We shall consider in turn lustre, ironstone china figures, Parian and transfer printed earthenware, though the account of each will be necessarily brief.

English lustre pottery is unmistakably English and unquestionably 'period'. If we apply the time-honoured test that requires a work of art to reflect its times, this metallized pottery fired at a low temperature emerges triumphant. We cannot claim it as an art however, and must be content to regard it as good vigorous pottery. It could not have been made anywhere but in England and there only in the early nineteenth century. Of the many types which flooded the markets of England and America during the first three or four decades of the nineteenth century the resist wares are by far the most interesting. Some of the charming and genteel patterns were eminently fitted for the drawing-room. Others, in the form of ale jugs, bearing prints copied from contemporary colour prints, were as obviously intended for the tavern. The facility of English lustre to mince with Miss Austen or to roister with Rowlandson endears it to the collector. There is, moreover, an historical importance attaching to the ware which is often overlooked. Lustre pottery with printed decoration has a strong documentary interest which evokes a whole social system now immeasurably remote. References to contemporary events and celebrities of the day, as well as pious quatrains or licentious doggerel, are used with a vigour that we cannot but admire in these days of enforced austerity. As with some contemporary printed earthenware, printed lustre achieves a 'literary' interest that is both instructive and amusing. Taken as a class, English lustre is all things to all men—it lacks only genuine wit. In a word, it is folk art applied to pottery.

In England the application of thin films of metal to pottery was due to the researches of Josiah Wedgwood. Probably as early as 1775 he was engaged in experimental work, evidently with the idea of imitating Near Eastern and Italian true lustres. From notes in the Wedgwood Museum at Barlaston it seems likely that he received assistance from his fellow members of the Royal Society but it is certain that other potters were engaged in the same task. Whatever the facts, it is evident that by 1790 or thereabouts some lustred earthenware was being made in the Potteries and by 1800 the production was considerable.

---

(1) *Plate* 17B; (2) *Plate* 17A; (3) *Plate* 14.

Broadly considered there are six classes of English lustre:—

1. Plain (either 'gold', 'silver' or 'copper').
2. Painted.
3. Resist.
4. Printed and banded in lustre.
5. Moulded in relief.
6. Stencilled.

Various combinations are known, such as blue prints with silver lustre embellishments and printed wares to which lustre painting has been added. Coloured grounds including the prized canary-yellow and a subtle apricot-buff are excellent. In the earlier specimens the body-material was usually creamware; white earthenware also was used and frequently, we find lustre on bone-china bodies. The makers were many, though few pieces are marked. Wedgwood, Hollins & Warburton, Aynsley, Lakin & Poole, Lockett, Riley, Bott, Wood & Caldwell, Wilson, Adams, Salt, E. Mayer, Meigh, Minton, Barker Sutton & Till, Copeland & Garratt and Bailey & Batkin are known to have made lustre. Lustre wares, with local characteristics, were made at Bristol, Sunderland, Newcastle-on-Tyne, Swansea, Herculaneum (Liverpool) and at the Yorkshire potteries. The homely copper lustre which continued almost to our own day was usually on a red body. Much of it was made for sale at country fairs. Old receipt books give us the rough and ready methods of preparing the lustre in the early nineteenth century and we learn that gold effects were obtained by dissolving the metal in aqua regia which was then mixed with sulphur and turpentine. Wedgwood produced a lustrous plum lustre from the purple of Cassius; 'silver' was obtained from the newly discovered platinum and the charming resist effect, undoubtedly the most attractive of all English lustres, was the result of painting out the pattern with glycerine or shellac in spirits of wine. After decoration, the ware was dipped in lustre and finally washed to remove the under painting or resist, which left the pattern in negative. The jugs (1) are examples of the free and attractive use of this process but the beaker in this illustration has been decorated in the positive manner by painting the lustre vine scrolls and the banding on to the body. The specimens (2) show this same linear freedom of brush work but here enamel colouring has been added for greater effect. The bird (right) is in enamel colours and although unsophisticated as is so often the case with peasant art, it has a charm of its own. The vases on square plinths (3) show lustre in combination with printed views as does the mug (4). These rustic scenes were often applied to coloured grounds of yellow,

---

(1) *Plates* 21c, E; (2) *Plate* 20A; (3) *Plate* 21A; (4) *Plate* 25c.

B. EARTHENWARE PLATE. MARK, 'WEDGWOOD' IMPRESSED
ETRURIA (WEDGWOOD'S FACTORY)
ABOUT 1840
DIAM. $8\frac{3}{8}$ IN.
See page 12

buff or light brown with charming effect. The plate (1) is evidence that much lustre pottery was made for presentation and many specimens bear dates of the early nineteenth century and often the house or farm name of the recipient.

Somewhat earlier in date are the plain silver lustres, the shapes of which recall the creamware of Wedgwood. These are coated with a wash of lustre, but so-called 'all over' effects are the least satisfactory of all English lustres as the resemblance to contemporary plated wares is so close as to suggest a desire to deceive.

Figures in lustre are not uncommon during the first half of the nineteenth century. Bailey & Batkin of Longton, Salt of Hanley, Wilson, and Wood & Caldwell are some of the known makers. The 'all over' effect on these figures is scarcely more successful than in the tea wares. Pink lustre was obtained from gold and some very beautiful patterns were produced by using it in combination with 'silver' and with enamel colours. On porcelain bodies it was particularly charming as will be seen from the examples on (2). The New Hall factory and Mintons of Stoke made some slightly decorated tea services between 1820 and 1830 which are as attractive as anything produced during the century (3). Lustre was used for the embellishment of printed wares at Sunderland and the spirited jugs and bowls are well known. These often bear prints of ships, and sailors indulging a maudlin farewell around which are scribbles of pink lustre and patches of cellular lustre of repulsive aspect.

With such a brave beginning it is surprising that lustre decoration had so little influence on the later wares of the century. Perhaps, as with slipware, lustred pottery is too near peasant art and the conditions under which it flourished, to have a place in our mechanistic civilization, but in our own time some attention has been paid to the method, especially at the Wedgwood factory where Alfred & Louise Powell worked in a particularly attractive style.

A fine white porcellanous ware for which the term 'pseudo-jasper' has been suggested, but more usually known as CASTLEFORD STONEWARE, was made at several potteries in England and Scotland from the earliest years of the century. The general appearance of the ware and especially the tasteful classical decoration in relief, invites comparison with the Wedgwood jaspers. We may therefore assume that Castleford ware was introduced as a substitute for jasper. Invariably well potted, sometimes translucent and, with the exception of Parian, almost the only nineteenth century ware that relies upon the beauty of an unglazed body, it is strange that Castleford did not

---

(1) *Plate* 21B; (2) *Plates* 20E, 24A, B; (3) *Plate* 20E.

achieve greater success (1). Several firms in North Staffordshire were engaged in its manufacture but the firm of David Dunderdale of Castleford in Yorkshire appears to have been the largest producer. The excellent white stoneware jugs of Turner and his contemporaries belong to the eighteenth century though they continued to be made during the first half of the nineteenth century. Somewhat akin to so-called Castleford was a grey-white stoneware often moulded in relief and bearing a smear glaze. It was not dipped in the usual way and the thin glaze effect was obtained by depositing raw glaze in the saggar or fire-box which volatilised in the heat of the kiln and settled on the ware. This ware, erroneously called salt-glaze, was made by Wedgwood, the Ridgway factories, Cockson & Harding, Walley of Cobridge and Stevenson of Cobridge among others. It is a trivial type of pottery not unlike the contemporary jet ware.

'IRONSTONE CHINA'. So-called ironstone china was distinctive and not particularly attractive but it was certainly a child of the nineteenth century and it possessed virtues that endeared it to the hearts and pockets of the Victorians. It was relatively cheap and well nigh indestructible. The discovery of this new pottery body took place early in the century but it is still doubtful how it came to be known. The patent granted to Turners in 1800 may have been the starting point of all the 'stone china' and 'semi-porcelain' bodies, or C. J. Mason may have been the inventor. The latter view appears most likely as many of the Turner plates and jugs are undoubtedly porcellanous. Indeed some of the better productions are translucent and it seems likely that the patent with its ingenuous rigmarole about Tabberner's mine rock is just an excuse for another slight variation upon the standard artificial body of the late eighteenth century. From its earliest days 'ironstone china' was handicapped by artless adaptations of *famille rose* and other late export Chinese wares which appear to owe their introduction to the Mason family. Early in the century, Miles Mason kept a shop in Fenchurch Street London, where Chinese pottery was sold and replacements provided and it seems likely that the stock patterns arose in this way. The Mason firm and their successors (G. L. Ashworth Bros.) remained true to this pseudo-Chinese decoration and succeeded in stamping ironstone china with a Sino-Anglican air that it never entirely lost (2). Essentially a utility ware, the best 'ironstone china' is seen in the massive dinner services, many of which are in daily use to-day (3). These were made of the original body which consists of China clay, china stone, flint, and bone ash, glazed with borax, flint and spar. Less interesting are the sets of jugs and ornaments—vases,

---

(1) *Plates* 28A, B; (2) *Plate* 29; (3) *Plate* 49.

bowls and so forth—the body of which contains little or no china clay and was whitened by the inclusion of enamel blue. The poorest wares made by other firms in emulation of Mason were often compounded of blue clay, stone and glass cullet, yet even these crude wares are not without interest as they are the progenitors of our excellent hotel wares of to-day.

FIGURES for decorative purposes were made throughout the century in earthenware, stoneware, Parian and porcelain. The earthenware figures of 1820–40 combine the primitive vigour found in the image toys of Astbury and Whieldon with a peculiarly Victorian feeling, hard to define, which many collectors find amusing. These figures were made by a school of back-street potters in North Staffordshire headed by John Walton (1790–1840) of Burslem. Few were original; many were crude copies of Derby porcelain with tree backgrounds, others were freely adapted from the better class figures of Enoch Wood. A distinctive class of equestrian figures probably from the Staffordshire potteries appeared about 1820. The potter has not been identified but the absurd figures on gaily prancing ponies—they are too small to pass as horses—and the joyous enamel colouring show him to have been a man of independent outlook. These chimney-piece ornaments of 1820–40, making no concession to refined taste, were intended for humble folk and were sold very cheaply to packmen for re-sale at country fairs. Those by Walton are by far the best but Ralph Hall of Tunstall, Salt of Hanley, J. Dale of Burslem, Edge & Grocott, Barker Sutton & Till and others produced similar wares (1). Mr. R. G. Haggar has recorded the names of many North Staffordshire figure makers. His researches into the directories and rate books have given the collector fresh potters to search for but it is unlikely that their work will be of merit.

Wasters recovered from excavations on the site of the Ralph Wood works at Burslem (2) suggest that the factory continued during the minority of Ralph Wood III (1781–1801). Jacob Tittensor who signed a plaque in 1789 may have had something to do with the factory as figures marked with his name are known. A more important potter of the early part of the century was Enoch Wood (1759–1840), a master potter in the truest sense of the term and a manufacturer of every kind of earthenware and porcelain. Early in life—it is said at the age of eighteen—he modelled a large plaque after the Antwerp 'Descent from the Cross' by Rubens. This extraordinary feat for one so young is to be seen in the old church at Burslem. As a modeller, Enoch Wood was competent but dull and his best works seem to have been portrait busts. His bust of John Wesley modelled in 1781 is uninspired but the

---

(1) *Plate* 35A; (2) *Plates* 33B, C.

Virgin and Child (1), if indeed it is by him, is excellent. This and several of his more ambitious creations have an air of adaptation and it is certain that he copied his well-known Bacchus and Ariadne from a 'Roman' marble formerly at Marbury Hall, Cheshire. In 1790 Enoch Wood took James Caldwell into partnership and until 1818 the mark of the factory was Wood & Caldwell but the latter was a sleeping partner only and the management of the works was the sole concern of Enoch Wood.

In the early days of the century some interesting figures were made at the Church works, Hanley, where Neale & Wilson had potted from 1789 to 1795. Robert Wilson who died in 1801 and David Wilson who carried the works on to 1816, the year of his death, made square base figures in a hard chalky body with slight decoration and others coated with platinum lustre. The brothers were makers of enamelled Toby jugs bearing an impressed crown on the base.

Excellent busts were made by Bott & Co. of Longton and at the Herculaneum works, Liverpool, which specialized in naval heroes and American celebrities. At the Sunderland works of Dixon Austin & Co., artless sets of the Seasons and other figures were made which seem to have been copied from Staffordshire models. Fell of Newcastle was a more original potter and his work possessed a certain naïve sincerity. Figures bearing the impressed mark of Wedgwood are often met with but it is certain that they were not made at the Etruria factory. Invoices from the Wood factory for the supply of figures in the white are known and it is likely that they were bought for decoration.

The potteries of Leeds and Swansea produced figures, some of which are original though, as at Sunderland, current Staffordshire best sellers were cheerfully pirated. In recent years, excellent figures bearing the names of potters as yet unknown have passed through the London sale rooms. Specimens marked A. Broom; Heath; Pattison and Barlow among others, point to a large production during the first forty years of the century.

About 1820 an interesting figure potter standing apart from the Walton and Wood schools was Obadiah Sherratt of Burslem who, when he was not borrowing from all and sundry, was capable of the bull baiting group 'Now Captin Lad' (2) and other amusing trifles. His work can be recognized by the high bracket feet upon which he mounted his groups. But all these little potworks cannot account for the very large number of 'Staffordshire' earthenware figures still in circulation and future research may prove that the Barker family of Longton was the most prolific of all. One of their works was near to

---

(1) *Plate* 31; (2) *Plate* 34B.

and ultimately absorbed the Sampson Smith concern to which reference will be made later. A branch of the Barker family became connected with the South Yorkshire potteries and Jewitt* tells us that Jesse and Peter Barker were at the Mexborough Old Pottery in 1804. Samuel the son of Jesse took over the Don pottery in 1834 and it is to this district that we must look for yet another class of figures belonging to the first half of the nineteenth century. These form a well marked group with sponged decoration on the bases in bright enamel colours and a distinctive modelling of children with disproportionately small heads. Toby jugs, groups for bedside use to take a pocket watch, cow cream jugs and milkmaid groups are not uncommon but never bear a mark. Closely similar groups usually with a central urn were made by David Wilson earlier in the century and revived by Shorthose but these are not in the sponged colours of Yorkshire, being decorated in blue only.

An even cheaper version of chimney-piece ornaments began to appear before 1850 and it is usual to refer them to Sampson Smith (1813–1878) of Longton though other makers are likely to have engaged in the manufacture (1). All pretence of modelling in the round has been abandoned, the backs being wrought in a summary fashion proving that they were intended for the mantelpiece. Some of the best figures of this class which have a quality of their own appeared in the 60's bearing decoration in rich underglaze blue with bright onglaze enamels. A brick red enamel and liquid gilding allied to a rich underglaze blue produces a very distinctive effect (2). A recent discovery of moulds at the factory suggests that figures were made as late as 1890.

Spirit flasks of buff earthenware bearing a dark brown 'Rockingham' glaze belong here. They are vigorously modelled and show a fanciful feeling strangely out of keeping with the times. Some flasks in the form of mermaids are quite foreign in conception and may have been copied from Continental faience. They are never marked but it is thought that they were made in South Yorkshire, Derbyshire, Staffordshire and the Jackfield district of Shropshire during the middle of the century. This so-called Rockingham glaze was extensively used on nineteenth century domestic wares and the term is always applied to a treacle-brown effect, but it is certain that the original glaze of the Rockingham factory at Swinton was quite different. A graceful jug in the Hanley Museum (3) marked 'Rockingham' bears a purplish-brown glaze of great charm.

---

* Jewitt, Llewellynn. *The Ceramic Art of Great Britain.* 1878.
(1) *Plate* 36; (2) *Plates* 36, 37A; (3) *Plate* 3B.

Figures of a very homely kind and almost certainly for local consumption were made in Scotland. Fisherwives, modelled in the Staffordshire style of 1820–30, were made by Thomas Rathbone & Co. of Portobello. A distinctive enamel decoration of yellow, orange, brown and dull green, together with underglaze cobalt, is found on these figures and on the similar productions of Prestonpans.

4

PARIAN WARE

Parian porcelain, originally compounded of felspar and china clay but later adulterated with ball clay and even flint glass, was used for figures. Introduced about 1840–45 by the Copeland & Garrett factory, who had been experimenting with a body material that would enable them to make use of the Derby figure moulds in their possession, it proved an excellent material for Victorian sentiment. Figures and groups of every size from small mantelpiece ornaments to ponderous statuettes two feet or more in height appeared at the Great Exhibition of 1851. The makers were legion and it is suggested that the Parian formula was common knowledge before 1840. Be this as it may, the following factories, among others, were producing some extraordinary figures and groups in the 50's: Mintons, Rose of Coalport, Wedgwood, Adams, Davenport, Worcester, Brownfield, Ridgway & Bates and Robinson & Leadbeater. Later, the material was used for hollow ware, with great ingenuity but little charm by the Belleek factory and by W. H. Goss of 'heraldic china' fame. At best an ivory body with a seductive surface somewhat greasy to the touch; at worst a hard chalky material not unlike bisque porcelain, it must certainly rank as a nineteenth century discovery. From about 1860 onwards some of the best figures in Parian were modelled by the French artists at Mintons and at the Cauldon works. But apart from such men as Jeannest, Hughues-Protat, Simeon and Carrier-Belleuse, few modellers were capable of more than an occasional success. It could not have been otherwise as models were commissioned from celebrated sculptors of the day who knew nothing of the peculiar difficulties attaching to ceramic modelling. Figures are known, often adapted by modellers at the factories, which bear the following names: John Bell, Count D'Orsay, Foley, Gibson, J. Durham, Mary Thorneycroft, McLean, Woolner, W. T. Theed, Westmacott and even the great Chantrey. Charles Toft of Mintons, a versatile artist who is remembered for his imitations of Henri Deux faience, was an excellent modeller as his bust of Wellington shows (I). The influence of these artists was

(I) *Plate 75.*

negligible. Instead of fathering a school of ceramic modelling that would compare with the work of the eighteenth century porcelain factories, only terracotta figures resulted (1). Much of the decoration that disfigures so many of our nineteenth century buildings was inspired by this movement, though the work of Rowland Morris and Mathew Elder, who modelled for Blanchard of Blackfriars Road, London, and the Blashfield works at Stamford has an appropriate bigness of feeling. Parian porcelain as a vehicle for figure modelling lacked personality. It had neither the heroic quality of true Parian marble nor the tactile charm of soft paste porcelain. In falling between these extremes it achieved an over-modelled sentimentality that we find disagreeable to-day. One or two essays in Victorian baroque by unrecorded artists and some charming figures of children by the Adams factory are interesting. An extraordinary group 'The Vision of the Red Crosse Knight' by Joseph Pitts (2) and some pretty figures (3) are perhaps the best things produced in Parian.

---

(1) *Plates* 79, 92B; (2) *Plate* 76; (3) *Plates* 77, 78.

5

BLUE-PRINTED AND OTHER TRANSFER-PRINTED POTTERY

This is a ceramic innovation for which England may claim the honour. It belongs to the nineteenth century, though the method was in use before 1765. Essentially a product of the industrial revolution, it was taken up with new enthusiasm about 1810. In 1827 the firm of Fourdrinier, makers of tissue-paper, moved their works from Hertfordshire to the Potteries in order to concentrate on the manufacture of transfer papers. Much depended on the quality of the paper, as it played the important role of transferring the pattern from the engraved plate to the surface of the pot. Briefly the procedure was as follows:—after the copper plate had been deeply engraved, an impression was taken in ceramic colour on damped tissue paper by means of a plate printing press. The impression was cut to fit the pottery vessel and rubbed on to it by hand by means of a flannel boss. The ware was dipped in water to remove the paper and fired either under or on to the glaze. Onglaze transfer printing was earliest in use, being practised in porcelain and earthenware in the second half of the eighteenth century, usually in black, blue, pink or brick red. A pleasant brown and a harsh purple are found on creamwares late in the century. Underglaze colours for printing began to make their appearance towards the end of the eighteenth century. Black, cobalt blue, brown, and perhaps pink were used before 1800 but the enormous quantity of 'blue prints' from about 1810 onwards, entitles us to regard this ware as a nineteenth century speciality. Other underglaze colours followed; orange from litharge and antimony, purple-brown known as 'mulberry' from manganese, cobalt and nitre, were in use before 1830. Later, chrome green and a hideous blue-green favoured by the Ridgway factory, and finally rose-pink, were pressed into the service of transfer printed pottery which had a great vogue in Europe and the Americas. The Pratt factory at Fenton was able to bring most of these colours into a polychrome underglaze printing in time for the Great Exhibition of 1851 (I). Even earlier the firm of Mayer of Dalehall,

---

(I) *Plate* 64A.

Burslem, used two or three underglaze colours together and the Cauldon factory (Brown, Westhead, Moore & Co.) produced some excellent prints in full colour during the Great Exhibition period. But it is the blue that engages our attention, not only for the excellence of craftsmanship, both of engraving and printing, but also for the many phases through which it passed between 1810 and 1850. An intense blue which is said to have originated at the Adams factory is very distinctive (1). Flown blue, a method of printing which softened the subject of the engraving was in use in many factories. A light blue usually found on delicately engraved patterns became popular in the 30's (2). Many of the engravings were by anonymous factory artists but engraving shops which had existed in the Potteries area before 1800 multiplied in number as the popularity of transfer printed wares increased. Ellis & Shirley, the Sergeant family, Brookes, Pedley, Mollatt, and Fennell were all respectable engravers who were able to undertake plates in almost any style. Very little of their work is, for this reason, either original or marked with strong individuality but there is character in the plates of James Cutts who designed for Wedgwood. He had a fantastic imagination comparable to that of Ravilious in our own day. Thomas Hordley who supplied the Ridgway and Wedgwood factories with some charming designs is also noteworthy. Patterns were extraordinarily diverse and varied from adaptations of illustrations in contemporary travel books to literal copies of K'ang Hsi blue and white patterns which Spode introduced about 1810. Charming as these latter are, they cannot but be disturbing to the connoisseur by reason of the alien material and method. Engravings of rustics, 'botanical sprays', Rowlandson illustrations (3) and views with marked preference for romantic ruins were all produced in quantity (4). These views were often framed in absurd wreaths of flowers and foliage but the result, so far from being ludicrous, is effective. The growing trade with America brought a host of American subjects for which collectors pay high prices to-day (5). A list of all the pottery firms engaged in transfer printing would be long and wearisome but mention must be made of the following who produced excellent wares in every style: Adams of Tunstall and Adams of Stoke-on-Trent, Wedgwood, Davenport, Stubbs, Clews, Rogers, Enoch Wood, and Minton. The following firms specialised in the American market:—Adams, Wedgwood, Copeland, Minton, Clews, Godwin, J. & J. Jackson, T. Mayer, Meigh, Mellor & Venables, The Ridgways, Stevenson, Stubbs, Wood & Caldwell and R. Hall. Exceptionally good wares were made by the Belle Vue

---

(1) *Plates* 39B, 41A, B; (2) *Plate* 43; (3) *Plate* 39B; (4) *Plates* 40, 41; (5) *Plates* 38B, 39A, 44A.

Pottery at Hull and an almost equally high standard is found on the blue printed pottery made by Herculaneum, Dillwyn & Co. of Swansea and the Brameld factory at Swinton. A charming use of transfer printing combined a brown print with washes of colour usually orange, red and green. The firm of Sewell and Donkin of St. Anthony's, Newcastle-on-Tyne and Shorthose & Co. of Hanley, specialised in this 'printed and filled in' ware. More important, though not necessarily more satisfying, was the accomplished printing in green, or black and yellow, (1) from the larger factories. Yellow printing on a brown ground was practised at Middlesbrough and Portobello evidently to compete with japanned metal. Artless nursery wares of some evocative charm were made about 1830 by firms in the Staffordshire potteries and Newcastle. These trifles, lightly printed on moulded plates, usually with nursery rhymes or with illustrations from children's books, are among the best wares made for the young in modern times. Many other varieties of printed pottery were introduced in the first half of the century but space does not permit mention of them all.

---

(1) *Plates* 44B, 45B.

6

PORCELAIN, CHIEFLY OF THE FIRST HALF OF THE CENTURY

Once the Napoleonic wars were over, England entered upon a period of relative prosperity. According to Trevelyan the manufacturing North was in full employment by 1825; exports rose from forty-nine to sixty-nine million pounds between the years 1820–1830. The new plutocracy created by this sudden access of wealth was not slow in deciding what it liked. Magnificence was the obvious aim of the costly porcelains of the next seventy years and an ideal for most of the cheaper productions. A kind of gross elegance is typical. Such porcelain as that illustrated in *Plates* 50, 51 and 52 shows more eloquently than any words this desire for grandeur and display. The Spode factory together with Worcester and Derby were the undisputed arbiters of early nineteenth century luxury porcelain. All these factories used a good body material, the potting was adequate and often accomplished but to our modern way of thinking the taste was lamentable.

Josiah Spode II (1754–1827) is usually credited with the perfection of the bone-china formula, perhaps as early as 1794, though much of the credit is often claimed for his father. This body material, a soft paste containing calcinated bone, was used for almost all of the later porcelains made in this country and it is remarkable how quickly the knowledge spread. By 1818, according to Parson & Bradshaw's Directory, twenty-two firms were making bone china in North Staffordshire. In the hands of Spode and certain of his contemporaries it possessed undeniable charm but, too often, it was over-decorated and the beauty of the paste was hidden. The shapes of the Spode tea wares were usually good as one would expect from a firm which had commenced business in earthenware but the decorative pieces, intended for the *nouveau riche*, were pretentious. Spode painting shared in the general taste of the times; fruit painters, most of them anonymous, achieved a style at once realistic and over-luscious. The flower-painters, too, favoured full-blown bunches usually containing one or more roses of monstrous growth. A speciality of the firm was a pleasant use of ground laying—a highly skilful method of providing a coloured background for decoration—and several exquisite colours were employed with good effect (1). The factory had a curious dual personality—excellent wares in typical English taste were made at the same time as garnitures of vases that are as foreign in appearance as anything ever produced in this country. The best porcelain produced by Spode in the grand manner during the early industrial period included tea services painted with subjects from natural history (2) and some remarkably ornate adaptations of French empire models.

DERBY, STAFFORDSHIRE AND WORCESTER

(a) Derby and Staffordshire

By 1800 seven of the porcelain factories that had brought a measure of fame to English ceramics in the previous century had come to an end. Longton Hall closed in 1760; Chelsea ceased to be independent and was closed in 1784. Bow and the rest came to an end between 1775 and 1800. Only three succeeded in surviving—Derby, Worcester and Caughley-Coalport. At Derby much fine porcelain continued to be made after 1800 and a somewhat amiable version of Wedgwood's classicism persisted until about 1830. Large sets of vases in this neo-classical taste, known for some reason as 'Campăna vases', were produced for wealthy folk. These vases were often hung with English, more rarely Continental, prospects, and painted in an elaborate minia-ture style deriving from the eighteenth century water-colourists (3). The brothers Brewer, drawing masters at Derby and pupils of Paul Sandby, were responsible for some of them. George Robertson and Jesse Mountford painted in a similar style which seems to have ori-ginated with Boreman in the previous century. It could be amusing, though hardly profitable, to distinguish the work of these and many other peripatetic view-painters. Without the evidence of paste, indeed, it is sometimes difficult to decide where a piece was made. Landscape painting as practised here, was imitated at Swansea, Pinxton and by Spode, Davenport and Enoch Wood. White wares painted in this style at the London decorating shops of Mortlock, Sims, J. Powell and Robin-son and Randall provide present-day collectors with never-ending problems of attribution. Later about 1850, a Staffordshire painter, Dan Lucas, went to Derby and produced some theatrical work owing much to contemporary oil painting; his style is unmistakable (4). The Derby flower painting at this time was patently in the romantic tradi-tion of William Billingsley (see pp. 29, 31 and 33). Much of the work was no more than a respectable imitation of the best Derby painting of 1780 but it was still of interest. John Brewer was a capable, though uninspired, flower-painter and much so-called Billingsley painting is

---

(1) *Plate* 61B; (2) *Plates* 56,57; (3) *Plate* 50; (4) *Plate* 73.

from his hand (1). The Steeles, father and two sons, made use of several manners, perhaps the best known being the highly finished fruit pieces of Thomas Steele senior (2). A younger son, Horatio, evolved a thin, highly-coloured style which became very popular at the Davenport and other factories in Staffordshire. His work can be recognized by the use of long-stemmed flower bunches often containing sprays of vetch. Figures were made in the early nineteenth century some of which were re-issues of the productions of the previous century. The new models were not of great importance. The later history of the Derby works is soon told: until 1811 Michael Kean was the proprietor. He was followed by Robert Bloor until 1826 and from thence until the factory closed in 1848, by a succession of managers. The present company was formed in 1876.

(b) Worcester

AT WORCESTER the firm of Flight and Barr was in possession of the old works at the commencement of the century. In 1840 the independent firm of Chamberlain absorbed the older company and in 1852, after various changes, Kerr and Binns took over until 1862 when the present Royal Worcester porcelain company was formed.

At Madeley in Shropshire imitations of Sèvres porcelain are thought to have been made about 1835 by a Coalport hand, T.M. Randall, who afterwards had something to do with similar productions at Mintons. Earlier in the century he had decorated white and sparsely decorated Sèvres porcelain which he bought from the Paris dealers.

The paramount influence in these concerns was that of the old Worcester factory where the colouristic tradition of Dr. Wall had not been forgotten. Even in the middle of the nineteenth century during the lean years of porcelain, Worcester managed to produce some excellent wares. The Flight & Barr productions, though technically indebted to the eighteenth century, were distinctive. Ostentation was as apparent here as at Derby and in Staffordshire, but a middle-class conservatism seems to have saved the factory from some of the worst errors of Bloor. Many of the triumphs of the preceding century were repeated often with a loss of vigour and even a lack of understanding. The flower painting in several styles does not call for comment as most of it achieved no more than a laborious naturalism, but some of the sprig patterns in a frankly formal manner are not without charm though they possess little originality.

From the beginning of the century 'Japan' patterns in blue, red and gold were made here as well as at Derby and the Staffordshire potteries. The inspiration was the so-called Imari porcelain from

---

(1) *Plate* 55D; (2) *Plate* 70.

C. PORCELAIN VASE. MARK, 'CHAMBERLAINS WORCESTER'
WRITTEN IN CRIMSON. ABOUT 1815
HEIGHT, 12 IN.
See page 29

Japan, at best an inferior style but thoroughly bad when applied to the export wares which found their way to this country in the eighteenth and nineteenth centuries. This wave of Orientalism, by no means the first to influence European porcelain, was but one of many that was to afflict the nineteenth century. The Minton 'Japan' patterns (1) are preferable to Derby and immeasurably better than the revolting Chamberlain versions which came later (2).

Clever figure painting was a feature of the better Worcester porcelain of the period and that in grey or sepia monochrome has a sorrowful charm that recalls the indefatigable Angelica Kauffman or the prints of Cipriani and Bartolozzi (3). Melancholy may be said to represent the mood of the years 1815–20. Perhaps the long-drawn quarrel between the King and Queen Caroline may have been the cause, for it is evident that public opinion was profoundly moved by this unhappy wrangle. Certainly some Minton and New Hall wares, decorated with black prints, had a direct reference to this affair.

James Pennington who completed his apprenticeship at Etruria in 1792 was the leading figure painter at Worcester and was one of the first of the 'classical' ceramic painters. He specialised in austere representations of Truth, Justice and the nobler virtues. This allegorical work is rather tedious and we turn to his domestic groups which have more appeal for us to-day (4). Another figure-hand with a pensive outlook was Thomas Baxter who had studied at the Royal Academy. His work, which is found also on Swansea porcelain (5) inspired a whole school of painters both here and elsewhere (6).

(c) Worcester Porcelain

THE CHAMBERLAIN WORKS AT WORCESTER (approx. 1796–1840) used a hard greyish porcelain which is often so dense as to resemble stone-china. Later this was improved but the heavy shapes dictated by the earlier paste remained. Robert Chamberlain, the founder, who had worked at the old Worcester factory in his early days, commenced about 1783 to decorate white wares from Caughley, New Hall and elsewhere. Evidently a good business man he secured Royal Patronage in 1816 which brought him orders for highly ornate services from the 'nobility and gentry'. An example of this type of ware is figured on *Plate 47*.

AT NANTGARW near Cardiff a porcelain factory with a small output was founded in 1812–13 by the restless William Billingsley (b. 1758) and his son-in-law, Samuel Walker. The former was the potter and decorator whilst Walker appears to have constructed the kilns and

---

(1) *Plate* 48B; (2) *Plate* 46B; (3) *Plate* 55A; (4) *Plate* 55C; (5) *Plate* 54A; (6) *Plate* 55A.

managed the business. For want of capital the venture was soon in difficulties and six months later William Weston Young became a partner. In turn draughtsman, surveyor, botanical artist, author, speculator and pottery artist, Young was evidently a man of boundless energy but he was unable to maintain the factory in solvency. In 1814 Billingsley and his partners were again in financial straits and the venture was transferred to the Cambrian pottery owned by Dillwyn at Swansea where porcelain of several types was made. At first the Billingsley formula was tried but wastage from the kiln was an ever-present difficulty, and various expedients were tried by Dillwyn in an endeavour to secure a commercially successful body. Billingsley was again at Nantgarw from 1817 to 1820 but success eluded him and in the latter year he left Wales for Coalport. Young then became sole proprietor, until the works finally closed in 1822.

Welsh porcelain is of three main types with several unimportant variations. First in date is the highly translucent soft paste of Billingsley, made at Nantgarw from 1812 to 1814 (1) and for a short time at Swansea. The more refractory Swansea body which shows a greenish translucency by transmitted light was made during 1815 to 1817. Specimens of this type are eagerly sought by present-day collectors who know it as 'duck-egg' porcelain. Lastly, from about 1817 onwards an inferior porcelain containing soapstone in place of bone-ash was introduced by Dillwyn. This rather featureless ware is usually marked with a trident, or crossed tridents and the name 'Swansea'. Simple wares of classical shape owing something to the contemporary Paris factories were made at Nantgarw. As will be expected from a pottery with wider resources, the Swansea factory aspired to grander things. The neo-classicism of Derby was adopted with enthusiasm: vases on square plinths with bands of soft gilding were made here, usually in the later and more manageable body (2). Cabinet tea services, again in classical taste with distinctive cup handles, are typical of the factory.

The flower painting on many of these wares was inspired by Billingsley who was a pottery painter of undoubted skill and great influence. Originally apprenticed at Derby he shared the fate, common to ceramic artists, of never continuing long in one place. From Derby he went to Pinxton and thence to Mansfield and Torksey near Gainsborough. Ever on the look-out for an opportunity to try out his soft paste body he was later at Wirksworth, Worcester, Nantgarw and finally Coalport where he died in 1828. In all these places he left behind him the memory of a beautiful but unworkable 'china body' and the tradition of a new kind of flower painting (3). His imitators

(1) *Plates* 58B, 59A, 60A; (2) *Plate* 59B; (3) *Plate* 60A.

are found at all the porcelain works of the nineteenth century and even to-day his method of wiping out the high lights in rose painting is still in use at Stoke-on-Trent. The remaining painters at the Welsh potteries are of little importance. Stiff flower sprays in the manner of current botanical magazines and doubtless copied from them provide a well-known Swansea type. Bird decoration in a similar style is also common and points to the contemporary interest in Natural History or, as the Victorians would have it, 'the wonders of nature'. Enthusiasts for Welsh porcelain profess to recognise the work of some twenty artists but much of it is trivial and often amateurish. The work of Evan Evans and his nephew David, both of whom painted wild flower bunches often with a central dog-rose, is easily recognised, as is the painting of a far more important decorator, William Pollard (1).

NEW HALL, EARLY MINTON AND OTHERS: From the above factories supplying the wealthy and middle classes we turn with some relief to those catering for working folk. Here again it will be seen that true originality was almost wholly absent. The inspiration was different as one would expect from wares circulating in the lowest price market. Motives found on slip ware and salt glazed pottery were tidied-up and used again. Not that the decorators were conscious copyists: a good deal of our unlettered art, especially the so-called peasant style, appears to lie dormant in our racial consciousness, ready to spring into fresh life when conditions are favourable. Some nineteenth century embroidery and the virile painting seen on canal barges are cases in point.

The cheaper domestic porcelain made in Staffordshire and else-where between 1800–1830 has much of this feeling. Simplicity was the distinguishing characteristic, a virtue that was achieved, not by deliberate intention, but by commercial necessity. Very little apart from ordinary tea and kitchen ware was produced, though some of the factories catered for special markets. Shapes were of a more simple kind than those of the costly wares and a strange illustration of working class conservatism is to be seen in the survival of tea cups without handles (2). Teapots and cream jugs were copied, almost exactly, from contemporary silver or plate (3). Occasionally, little masterpieces of true peasant design were produced at the New Hall factory of Hollins Warburton & Co. (4) and at Mintons where an anonymous decorator worked in a curiously attractive oriental style (5). The term 'New Hall' has come to be accepted as a label for all this unsophisticated china but it is certain that much of it was made elsewhere. Minton, Davenport, Mason, Chamberlain and Caughley among others are

_____

(1) *Plate* 59B; (2) *Plate* 9A; (3) *Plates* 8B, C; (4) *Plate* 10B; (5) *Plates* 8A, B, 55B.

known to have produced similar wares. At Wirksworth in Derbyshire closely similar porcelain was produced after 1800 for a few years. Wasters from the site indicate that New Hall was imitated both in shape and decoration.

The early history of the New Hall company belongs to the eighteenth century when a true hard paste porcelain appears to have been made for a short time at Tunstall. In 1782 the company moved to the Hollins & Warburton works at Shelton and thenceforward until about 1801 large quantities of hardish grey porcelain were made and decorated with free adaptations from Chinese export wares, but it was not true hard paste in the Chinese or Meissen sense. In 1801 John Daniel, a capable potter, was taken into partnership and a commencement was made with the production of bone-china. This ware is sometimes marked with the name 'New Hall' in a double circle (1). The old hard body was not abandoned, however, for an invoice of 1812 speaks of 'real china', but the current Staffordshire bone-china idiom was not to be denied and by 1815 or thereabouts the production of the early paste had ceased. Charming sprig, festoon and 'chinoiserie' tea services in clean bright colour were made in quantity both in porcelain and earthenware. A curious decoration on the handles of teapots and cream jugs consisting of a series of dots and an outspread fan, usually in red, is typical of the Hollins Warburton factory. Towards the end of the early period the factory adopted Sèvres designs, apparently with no little success, for these patterns are found also on bone-china. In 1810 Peter Warburton, a brilliant potter, whose name might have been written large in ceramic history but for his early death, took out a patent for printed decoration in gold (2). Good engravings of scenery or rural pursuits, sometimes in gold or monochrome purple but more often washed over in crude colour, were a feature of late 'New Hall' (3). In 1831 the firm of Hollins Warburton & Daniel closed. What became of the pattern books is not known but at least one earthenware firm (perhaps Cockson & Harding who were later at the New Hall works) reproduced the pink ribbon and rosebud patterns on cheap earthenware services.

At Pinxton in Derbyshire a porcelain, often mis-shapen but oddly attractive, was made by Billingsley from 1796 until about 1810. Decoration emulated Derby in the important services, landscapes being especially frequent. A yellow ground, similar to that used at Derby, is seen on the better productions and some artless painting in purple is very characteristic of the factory. A curious 'stained glass' design consisting of lozenges and squares of contrasting colours which has been

---

(1) *Plates* 10A, C; (2) *Plate* 18B; (3) *Plate* 19B.

ascribed to Torksey and to Wirksworth, seems to have emanated from Pinxton, as did some painting of named English birds by a hand who afterwards worked for Davenport. The factory closed in 1813.

ROCKINGHAM: The porcelain made on the *Rockingham* estate near Swinton in Yorkshire has neither the charm nor the incompetence of Pinxton. An earthenware factory had existed here from the second half of the nineteenth century but between 1820 and 1842 almost every kind of pottery and porcelain was being produced under the patronage of Earl Fitzwilliam. Bone-china of the Staffordshire type, decorated with loosely grouped flowers, was made in quantity. Tea services with charming grounds of buff, grey or green and lace-work gilding, achieved wide popularity. Simple figures of some interest and incredible vases showing great potting skill but abominable taste are well-known productions of the factory. A considerable interchange with Derby, both of workmen and artists, gives to much Rockingham porcelain, perhaps unjustly, an air of having been copied from the midland factory (1).

The Rockingham factory, together with Spode, may be said to express the Regency spirit in decorated porcelain. At *Coalport*, however, a large and important factory pursued an even course throughout the century. It was untroubled by fashion and, with the exception of French models which were always admired, largely uninfluenced by other factories. Founded by John Rose towards the end of the eighteenth century, the Coalport company acquired Caughley in 1799 and the Billingsley formula in 1819. The mark CBD or, more rarely, 'Coalbrookdale', which appears on some Coalport porcelain has not been explained satisfactorily and it is suggested that the amalgamating activities of Rose included a decorating establishment at this place (2). In 1820 Rose was awarded a medal for a leadless felspathic glaze and ten years later he was producing a fine, translucent body which obviously derives from the Billingsley formula. Factory marks are not common on early nineteenth century Coalport and much fine porcelain with moulded patterns is often claimed for Nantgarw or Swansea. Coalport had a distinctive style, however, as will be seen from *Plates* 63A and B. Flower painting in a palette of bright colours was practised at the factory by William Cook, among others, and a heavy version of Billingsley's rose painting was for long popular (3). The combination of this florid painting with modelled and applied decoration is overpowering, but typical of the period 1830–50. About the time of the Great Exhibition some careful copies of Sèvres and Chelsea were produced (4). The factory was not concerned wholly with elaborate wares however and

(1) *Plate* 52; (2) *Plate* 65A; (3) *Plate* 62A; (4) *Plate* 68.

some slightly patterned tea services of the 50's are very pleasant. Coloured grounds including an acid green, and *rose Pompadour*, were a speciality of the factory. Rose died in 1841 but the firm persisted throughout the century until it became amalgamated with one of the Staffordshire pottery concerns in our own day.

The important firm of Davenport of Longport in Staffordshire made every kind of pottery and porcelain until 1882. Bone china was the usual body material but a hard grey paste, not unlike that of Chamberlain of Worcester, was sometimes used. Decoration varied from copies of Ch'ien Lung designs to flower painting in the Derby manner (1). Many painters of the first half of the century seem to have travelled from Derby to the Davenport works and back again to Derby. A painter who specialised in bouquets of large pink roses worked for both factories as well as for Spode (2). This may be Thomas Steele (see also *Plate* 70). Jesse Mountford, a landscape painter from Derby, was at Longport and Joshua Cristall the water-colour painter is said, on unproved tradition, to have been apprenticed at the works.

Of the lesser factories little need be said. Much of the cheaper porcelain was made by small firms who are now forgotten though the factories may still exist. During the first half of the nineteenth century many small pot-banks changed hands, often without record, for trifling sums. A careful and hard working artisan could save sufficient money to buy a derelict pot works by the time he was forty. In 1834, for instance, a Cobridge pot works belonging to a member of the Adams family was sold for £253 and the bill of sale sets forth the following:— an oven, a throwing house, a turning house, a sliphouse, a hot house, a saggar shed and a lead house, together with a modelling shop and a printing house, to say nothing of clay, tools, moulds, utensils but, apparently, no machinery. These pottery works do not always appear in the Directories and even when they do we are quite without information regarding their productions. Many of their wares are still in circulation and present the humble collector with an opportunity for wishful thinking, especially as so few are marked. Inevitably, as time passes, such things tend to become identified with the better-known factories.

The enormous pottery works of JOB, WILLIAM & EDWARD RIDGWAY, occupying seven or eight factories in North Staffordshire, produced every kind of pottery and porcelain. The Ridgways, moreover, were concerned in pottery making in other parts of England—at Hull and Poole—and they traded in potters' materials also. At the Cauldon works, John Ridgway who succeeded his father Job in 1814 made some excellent bone china up to 1859. The factory was evidently in

---

(1) *Plate* 69; (2) *Plate* 58.

D. PORCELAIN VASE. COALPORT
ABOUT 1855
HEIGHT, 11 IN.
See pages 33, 34

competition with Herbert Minton for, from 1845 onwards, a number of French artists was employed whose work is similar to that of the Minton artists. The later history of Cauldon is interesting as under Brown, Westhead, Moore & Co. increasingly elaborate services of porcelain were produced. The porcelain figures of about 1865 (1) have a curious feeling that recalls Astbury and Whieldon.

MISCELLANEOUS

MILES MASON (1752–1822) a potter with an independent turn of mind, who seems to have received his early training at Worcester, made several types of porcelain early in the century. His earliest wares were in a hard grey body which resembles New Hall (2). The decoration, too, was adapted from Chinese export wares. Mason started with his version of bone-china about 1815. Technically this was a most successful material for we find almost complete tea services by him in use to-day. This ware is usually marked with an imitation Chinese seal character.

The well-known firm of Wedgwood made porcelain for a few years from 1812. Cutts, who had worked at Pinxton, painted landscapes on porcelain for Wedgwood in a style that recalls some of the lesser Derby painters. These laborious views became very popular in Staffordshire and at the Mason factory (3). Davenport and Enoch Wood (4), among others, produced quantities of porcelain bearing this kind of decoration. Indifferent bird studies not unlike the work of Colclough of Swansea and some curious Chinese patterns in green are known, bearing the mark 'Wedgwood' in red. About 1812 the firm purchased publisher's copper plates and used them for porcelain decoration, as the figure numbers show (5). But little else of the period 1812–16 is of interest and one cannot resist the feeling that porcelain was regarded as an alien material at Etruria. Riley of Burslem did rather better and some of his domestic wares suggest that he had a knowledge of the tin enamel glaze for porcelain which had been used at Liverpool in the previous century. He was, moreover, engaged in experiments with a body material rather like Parian, as an ugly little jug at Hanley proves. This jug, dated 1823, is moulded in relief and decorated in onglaze enamel colours (6).

Some forthright but tasteless porcelain was made between 1830 and 1850 by many small firms in North Staffordshire. Shorthose & Co. of Hanley made competent tea wares with blue decoration rather like Caughley; the firm of Hilditch & Sons of Longton was similar and

(1) *Plate* 37B; (2) *Plate* 11A; (3) *Plate* 11A; (4) *Plate* 16B; (5) *Plate* 9C; (6) *Plate* 28C.

some of their printed wares are well potted though both firms were really earthenware manufacturers who had turned to porcelain production. Curious chimney ornaments in a glassy porcelain not unlike Longton Hall were made by Carey & Co. of Fenton and a large output of wares of every kind, mostly in emulation of Derby, was maintained by Mayer & Newbold, Enoch Wood, Jesse Breeze of Tunstall and Charles Bourne of the Foley, Fenton. The large factory of Adams at Stoke-on-Trent favoured Worcester patterns on a material which is often indistinguishable from the current productions of Grainger & Co. (1839–89) of Worcester.

THE HERCULANEUM FACTORY AT LIVERPOOL was active from 1796 to 1841 during which time immense quantities of earthenware and porcelain were made, much of it for the North American markets. Shapes and decoration favoured current Staffordshire wares as might be expected from a factory employing workmen from Stoke-on-Trent. Fine bat-printing was practised here as will be seen from *Plate* 19A, though this example is on an earthenware body.

7

THE GREAT EXHIBITIONS
(1840-1870)

When in the nineteenth century, and for the first time in our history, we developed a taste for applied art, the standard was anything but high. Almost every single factor since the late mediaeval period had conspired to deprive us of the materials for a truly national art. Simple craftsmanship was always evident, as has been said, but when the craftsman turned to decoration the results were unfortunate. He had no school training upon which to draw and the attraction of intricate models proved irresistible. Foreign styles were greatly admired in the pottery industry from 1840 onwards and every endeavour was made to copy ornamental wares as exactly as possible. The Great Exhibition of 1851 which brought many of these influences together had the effect of making manufacturers and the public exhibition-conscious. Every few years international *expositions* were arranged in Europe and America to which the large pottery firms were only too glad to contribute. This cult of the exhibition was as bad for pottery design as the contemporary water-colour exhibitions were for painting. Wares were designed to excite astonishment or to encourage distinguished patronage and many absurd objects were produced. Technical ability of a very high order was employed on badly designed vessels which often were loaded with meaningless decoration. The fundamentals of a good ceramic approach were disregarded. With an almost complete mastery of material came a feeling of elation; nothing was felt to be beyond the powers of the potter and we find some of the important factories imitating wood, marble, metal (1) and even marquetry (2), in their desire to impress.

Furthermore the foundation of the Victoria and Albert Museum in 1844, admittedly with the soundest intentions, had an unexpected effect. Period decoration became fashionable and simple good sense became *démodé* and was left to the smaller factories. French Renaissance art in particular was felt to be desirable and a vogue that owed its introduction to Mintons commenced about 1860.

(1) *Plate* 87; (2) *Plate* 86.

D
37

8

MINTONS

This firm which dominated English ceramics from 1840 as thoroughly as Wedgwood had done fifty years before, became a veritable branch of the Sèvres manufactory in matters of taste. French artists were brought to the works and a colony, the remnants of which remain to this day, was set up in Stoke-on-Trent. Among the earliest to arrive were Hughues-Protat, Carrier-Belleuse, the master of Rodin and Victor Simeon—all sculptors. Mussill, a Czech from Altrohlau, and Leroy and Henk from Sèvres soon followed. The Franco-Prussian war of 1870 brought many painters to Staffordshire including some highly gifted men of whom M. L. Solon was noteworthy, as he introduced a new technique to England from Sèvres. This was the *pâtes d'application* or *pâte sur pâte* to be mentioned later. Jahn, a figure painter from Vienna, arrived in 1862 and Lessore, a pupil of Ingres, with a facile style of drawing quite unlike that of his master, left Sèvres about the same time (1). Other artists of undeniable merit were Besche, Richgitz, Reuter and the popular A. Boullemier. Their work, usually on vases of French design, is sedulously collected in the Stoke-on-Trent area to-day. These French artists in addition to working at the factories of Minton, Copeland, Cauldon Place and Wedgwood, taught in the schools and a number of local men were able to profit from sound training. When they failed to provide work that was acceptable at the exhibitions, designs were commissioned from celebrated easel painters of the day. Alfred Stevens prepared some maiolica designs for Mintons which show little of his genius. H. J. Poynter, Walter Crane and the popular Stacey Marks and many others also were employed.

Mintons was the leading firm of the period, under the guidance of Herbert M. Minton (1793–1858), son of the founder of the firm. Herbert Minton was a man of vision and with the aid of Leon Arnoux, who came to Staffordshire from France in 1848, he produced a variety of wares of high quality. From 1850 to 1870 the factory maintained a large output of almost every kind of pottery and porcelain. Excellent tiles were made by the Prosser method. The Duke of Sutherland, who acted as a patron, lent specimens of his Sèvres porcelain which were

(1) *Plate* 80.

copied at the factory (1). He used his social connections to obtain loans of maiolica, Palissy ware (2) and specimens of the faience d'orion of Henri Deux which were also copied with great exactness. The factory painters were welcomed at Trentham, and Mussill and his assistant Pilsbury spent long hours in the conservatories where they made remarkable gouache studies which were used afterwards in the decoration of vases. This air of the hot-house pervades much of the Minton painting of 1860–75. Services of porcelain with elaborate centre-pieces were made at Mintons and exhibited in London at the showrooms of Mortlock & Co., Phillips & Co., and Goode of South Audley Street (3).

'Majolica', the absurd name given to colour glazed-pottery by the Victorian potter, was introduced by Mintons about 1850, primarily for decorative wares. Later it was used for domestic utensils and as a building material for the facing of staircases and balconies. Long before Whieldon made his tortoiseshell wares English potters were experimenting with glaze effects. Josiah Wedgwood in his list of Burslem Potters of 1710–15 gives eleven makers of mottled wares. The Ralph Woods, father and son, were masters of a repertoire of colour-glazes which they used with great skill in the closing years of the eighteenth century. Wedgwood himself introduced a green glaze and during the first half of the nineteenth century new glaze colours became available. These were used on a cane body in a very effective way by Mintons, Wedgwood and others. Little figures in caneware which were taken from porcelain moulds bear 'majolica' glazes. The effect is by no means unpleasing (4).

All the important factories vied in producing elaborate wares and each had its own speciality. The Copeland factory excelled in realistic flower painting; roses were recognisable as named varieties and good painting in several styles was done at the factory under the inspiration of C. F. Hurten. An amusing fashion for 'Grecian' pottery made its appearance about the time of the Great Exhibition. Bell of Glasgow, Dillwyn of Swansea and Pountney of Bristol made careful copies of Greek vessels bearing oddly inappropriate decoration. The firm of Alcock of Hilltop, Burslem, appeared to realise the futility of this antiquarianism and issued a series of Greek subjects in riotous colour. This enthusiasm for historic style led to some absurd errors of taste; the oenochoe was wedded to a basin for toilet purposes; Amerindian water-pots appeared as ornaments for the sideboard. The reconstructed porcelain factories at Worcester and Derby produced some miracles of misapplied craftsmanship. George Owen of Worcester was responsible for some extraordinary feats in pierced porcelain which emulated

---

(1) *Plates* 66, 67; (2) *Plate* 83; (3) *Plate* 65B; (4) *Plates* 82A, B.

Japanese ivory carving. Japanese pottery, especially export Satsuma, was highly thought of at Worcester, and many wares in the seventies and eighties have a pronounced Japanese feeling. Gothic wares were produced at the Old Hall factory of Meigh & Co. and it is a little surprising that no enterprising firm thought of giving the world designs in Japanese Gothic.

9

THE CLOSE OF THE CENTURY

The gospel of good design and restrained decoration formulated by William Morris and others began to gain converts in the pottery industry in the 80's. The results were not very robust and did not last long in popular favour but the work of the Bodley factory at Burslem and Henry Tooth at Bretby and Swadlincote deserve passing mention. At Birkenhead, the firm of Rathbone, trading as the De la Robbia pottery, produced some well modelled placques decorated with 'majolica' glazes. Other 'art' potteries flourished wherever suitable clay could be found. At Watcombe and Allervale in Devonshire terra-cotta wares were made in the closing years of the century which were artistic in intention. At the MacIntyre factory, Burslem, William Moorcroft did some excellent work in tube-lined slip, a modern equivalent of the old Staffordshire tradition. He later went into potting on his own account and became deservedly successful. William de Morgan derived from the aesthetic movement of William Morris and was especially enamoured of Persian pottery which he copied or adapted in strong colours and lustres (1). From about 1870 until 1890 T. J. Bott painted in white slip on dark blue-ground porcelain for the Worcester factory. His obvious inspiration was Limoges enamel (2). A more important artist was Marc Louis Solon who worked in a similar technique but with much greater accomplishment for the Minton factory. The method which he brought with him from Sèvres involved both painting and modelling in translucent white or tinted porcelain slip on a stained Parian body (3). He was an accomplished decorator and the father of a small school of artists at Mintons which included Fred Rhead, Hollins (4) and Alboin Birks. Solon became the author of several works on English and Continental pottery and Rhead has left us a charmingly gossipy book on Staffordshire pots and potters (*see* Bibliography).

The School of Art at Lambeth gave rise to a distinct movement in the late nineteenth century which produced the brown stonewares of Doulton and the Martin brothers. Under the tuition of C. L. Sparkes who was head of the school from 1856 a number of pottery artists were

---

(1) *Plates* 94, 95; (2) *Plates* 72, 85A; (3) *Plate* 85B; (4) *Plate* 84B.

trained at the Lambeth School, some of whom attained celebrity in their day. At the Doulton works John Broad with a monumental style and George Tinworth who specialized in religious subjects were competent modellers. Harradine, another talented figure modeller, borrowed ideas from Constantin Meunier and translated the heroic labourers of the Belgian artist into stoneware. The stoneware at the Doulton factory with its rugged salt glaze of a pleasant brown colour was eminently suited to small figure modelling: perhaps the best work of all was by M. V. Marshall who had a pleasant style. In much of his work he exhibited a real understanding of one aspect of *art nouveau* (1). Drawing on the clay was practised at Doultons by several artists who had been trained at the Lambeth School of Art. The work of Hannah Barlow is typical of this type (2), but her sister Florence and others worked in a similar style. Henry Simeon designed some excellent shapes (3) and also decorated vases in a manner indistinguishable from that used by F. C. Pope (4). A more important artist was Léon, son of Marc Louis Solon who modelled figures and placques at Mintons and painted in a very distinctive style for the firm and for Pilkingtons Tile Works at Manchester. He was the ceramic Beardsley (5).

Opinion is sharply divided upon the merits of the Martin brothers. To some tastes the brown stoneware grotesques made at Fulham and Southall from 1873 to 1912 are disturbing. There is, however, a strong clay feeling about much of the work of the Martins though their sombre hollow wares made in the twentieth century under the influence of Japanese tea wares, are to be preferred to the earlier fantasies. But for good or ill the name of Martin conjures up the strange, half-humorous birds which will always be admired by collectors (6). It is often asserted that these three brothers were the earliest of the studio potters. That they worked in a studio atmosphere is, of course, quite true but they were more directly akin to the craftsman. The craft of brown stoneware which had been long settled in the London area persisted throughout the century (*see* page 8) and it is to this tradition rather than to the artist-potter connection that they belong. The artist-potter proper was already stirring towards the end of the nineteenth century but it was not until after 1900 that studio pottery was produced in any quantity. Other *fin de siècle* activities included the interest that was being taken in France and England in the high temperature glazes of China. In this country the work of Bernard Moore in association with William Burton was directed towards the monochrome copper reds and flambé glazes. Moore used a bone china body at first and his

(1) *Plate* 93B; (2) *Plate* 88; (3) *Plates* 92A, C; (4) *Plate* 93A; (5) *Plate* 92B; (6) *Plates* 90, 91.

pottery has a pleasant lacquer effect quite unlike the Chinese glazes which he sought to imitate (1). Later, when he came to realise the importance of body material and used a hard paste, his success was striking (2). He experimented also with lustre and became master of a wide variety of glaze effects which, though not original, were of importance in the history of nineteenth century ceramics. Somewhat similar research was being pursued at the tile factories of Pilkingtons of Manchester, Maw & Co. of Broseley, and Godwin & Thynne of Hereford principally in the direction of true high temperature lustres.

At the Ruskin pottery, West Smethwick, Birmingham, Edward Richard and Howson Taylor experimented with glaze effects most of which were in emulation of Chinese wares (3). The best were produced after the death of Edward Richard Taylor in 1912 and thus belong to the twentieth century but the Ruskin pottery is another illustration of the scientific approach to ceramics that arose in the period 1890–1900.

Lithophanes which exploited the translucency of porcelain were made by a few English factories working under licence from Griffith Jones of London who had acquired the method from the French inventor. Plaques, lampshades and tea wares were made by this method which had a certain affinity with the *émail ombrant* of Rubelles, used by the Wedgwood factory about 1860. The lithophanes, however, bore colourless glazes over a modelled design whereas the Rubelles invention, which involved the use of colour-glazes, appears to have been produced by pressure. Mintons, Grainger & Lee of Worcester, Adderley & Lawson, the South Wales pottery at Llanelly and Copelands (4) are known to have made lithophanes.

Art nouveau derives, however indirectly, from one aspect of the teachings of William Morris. His healthy preoccupation with curved and re-curved plant form became a disease in the hands of the metal workers and wood workers of the 'nineties. Pottery and porcelain designs inspired by this fashion were never so extravagant, however, and some pleasant tea wares from the Staffordshire potteries exploited *art nouveau* for a short time in the 'nineties.

The inventiveness of the nineteenth century potter in the spheres of materials, decoration and process, is unquestionable. His successes entitle him to an honourable place in ceramic history.

---

(1) *Plate* 96A; (2) *Plate* 96B; (3) *Plate* 96C; (4) *Plate* 71.

MARKS

1. GENERAL

Nineteenth-century pottery and porcelain marks are of three types. (a) the factory mark (b) the pattern mark and (c) the artist's signature found on artistic wares in the last half of the century. Marks (a) and (b) are often found together as are marks (a) and (c). Engraved back-stamps, or 'semis', are found on transfer printed wares and ironstone china. Most nineteenth-century pottery back-stamps are self-explanatory. The following marks are not so readily understood.

2. REGISTRY MARKS

From 1842 to 1883 the British Patent Office employed a Registry mark on English registered manufactured goods of all kinds. The following tables will be found useful:

Index to the Letters for each month and year from 1842 to 1867

Year		Month	
1842	X	January	C
1843	H	February	G
1844	C	March, 1845	W
1845	A	April	H
1846	I	May	E
1847	F	June	M
1848	U	July	I
1849	S	August	R
1850	V	September	D
1851	P	October	B
1852	D	November	K
1853	Y	December	A
1854	J		
1855	E		
1856	L		
1857	K		
1858	B		
1859	M		
1860	Z		
1861	R		
1862	O		
1863	G		
1864	N		
1865	W		
1866	Q		
1867	T		

Letter R used from 1st to 19th September, 1857.

? Letter K used in December, 1860.

Index to the Letters for each month and year from
1868 (when Registry mark changed) to 1883

Year		Month	
1868	X	January	C
1868	H	February	G
1870	C	March	W
1871	A	April	H
1872	I	May	E
1873	F	June	M
1874	U	July	I
1875	S	August	R
1876	V	September	D
1877	P	October	B
1878	D	November	K
1879	Y	December	A
1880	J		
1881	E		
1882	L		
1883	K		

3. WEDGWOOD. DATE MARKS ON EARTHENWARE

The Wedgwood Factory introduced a system of date marking in 1860 which consisted of three capital letters: the first indicating the month, the second being the Potter's mark, and the third the year in which the piece was made.

The monthly marks from 1860 to 1864 are as follows:

January	J	April	A	July	V	October	O
February	F	May	Y	August	W	November	N
March	M	June	T	September	S	December	D

From 1864 to 1907 these monthly marks were changed to the following:

January	J	April	A	July	L	October	O
February	F	May	M	August	W	November	N
March	R	June	T	September	S	December	D

Year marks from 1860 to 1897 were in two cycles beginning with the letter O for 1860 and continuing through the alphabet in sequence to Z for 1871.

A second cycle began with A for 1872 and went to Z for 1897.

For permission to reproduce the above, grateful thanks are accorded to Messrs. Josiah Wedgwood & Sons Ltd.

4. MINTON MARKS

Impressed or painted on porcelain, parian, and caneware.

Number 3 painted in enamel colours, usually
blue, is an early nineteenth century mark.

Yearly Marks 1842–1897

1842	1843	1844	1845	1846	1847	1848	1849
✳	△	☐	✕	⬭	⌒	—	⋈
1850	**1851**	**1852**	**1853**	**1854**	**1855**	**1856**	**1857**
♧	∵	V	⌓	℔	✳	⚲	◇
1858	**1859**	**1860**	**1861**	**1862**	**1863**	**1864**	**1865**
♈	Ⅺ	♌	人	♱	⬙	Z	〰
1866	**1867**	**1868**	**1869**	**1870**	**1871**	**1872**	**1873**
X	⋇	⬓	⊡	Ⓜ	Ⅸ	⊗	✕
1874	**1875**	**1876**	**1877**	**1878**	**1879**	**1880**	**1881**
↓	Ɛ	⊿	◎	△	△	△	⊞
1882	**1883**	**1884**	**1885**	**1886**	**1887**	**1888**	**1889**
⊗	◷	⊠	⋈	B	♕	∞	S
1890	**1891**	**1892**	**1893**	**1894**	**1895**	**1896**	**1897**
T	①shield	②shield	③shield	④shield	swan 1	swan 2	swan 3

For permission to reproduce the above, grateful thanks are accorded to Messrs.
Mintons Ltd.

5. MISCELLANEOUS FACTORY AND OTHER MARKS

1. *Derby* until about 1810. 2. Bloor period 1811–1848. 3. Bloor period (late). 4. Stevenson (or Sampson) Hancock 1850–70. 5. The Royal Crown Derby Company founded 1876. 6. Tripod mark occasionally found on early nineteenth-century Derby porcelain. 7. *Pinxton*. 8. *Coalport*. 9. *Swansea*. 10. *Worcester*. Barr Flight and Barr. 11. Flight Barr & Barr. 12. Incised mark used at Worcester in the early years of the nineteenth century. 13. The Royal Worcester porcelain Company founded in 1862. 14. James Hadley & Co., Worcester founded in 1896. 15. Herculaneum Liverpool.

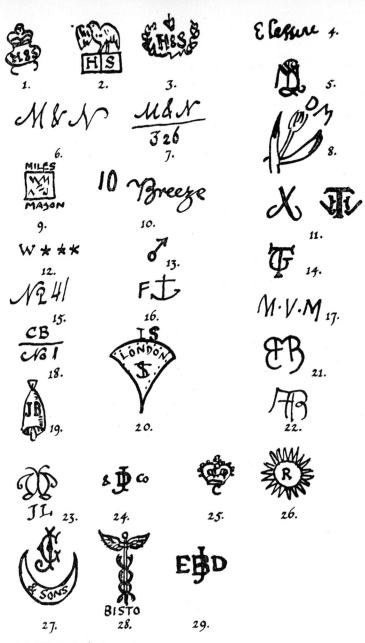

1, 2 and 3. Hilditch & Sons, Longton, about 1815. 4. Emile Lessore on Wedgwood wares. 5. Marc Louis Solon. 6 and 7. Mayer and Newbold, Lane End, about 1835. 8. William de Morgan. 9. Miles Mason. 10. Jesse Breeze, Greenfield, Tunstall (on porcelain, about 1830). 11. Howson Taylor. 12. Enoch Wood impressed mark on porcelain figures and bulb pots. 13. J. & J. Rogers, Longport. on porcelain. 14. George Tinworth (Doulton). 15. A typical New Hall (Hollins & Warburton) pattern mark. 16. Thomas Fell & Co., Newcastle-on-Tyne. 17. M. V. Marshall (Doulton). 18. Charles Bourne, the Foley (on porcelain). 19. Bell & Co., Glasgow. 20. On pink lustre? Middlesborough. 21. Hannah Barlow (Doulton). 22. Florence Barlow (Doulton). 23 and 24. J. Dimmock & Co., Hanley. 25. Wilson, Hanley. 26. Ratcliffe & Co., New Hall. 27. George Jones & Sons, Stoke on Trent. 28. Bishop, Hanley. 29. E. J. Stonier, Bodley, Burslem.

1, 2 and 3. Hicks and Meigh, Hanley 1806–22. 4. Andrew Stevenson, Cobridge 1816–36. 5. Job, Meigh & Son, Hanley 1820. 6. Hicks, Meigh & Johnson, Hanley 1822–36. 7. Thomas Carey & Sons, Fenton, 1826–41. 8. Cork and Edge, Burslem, 1831–64. 9. William Ridgway & Co., Hanley, Bell Works, 1830–54; Hanley, Church Works, 1834–6. 10 and 11. John Ridgway, Cauldonplace 1834–40. 12 and 13. Charles Meigh, Hanley 1835–47. 14. William Ridgway, several works in Shelton and Hanley 1835–56.

15 and 16. F. & R. Pratt & Co., Fenton 1840–1916. 17. C. & W. K. Harvey, Longton 1841–53. 18 and 19. Ridgway & Morley, Shelton 1842–4. 20. Hackwood & Co., New Hall 1842–56. 21. Francis Morley & Co., 1845–58. 22. W. & Joseph Harding, New Hall 1846–49. 23. W. Hackwood & Sons, New Hall 1846–50. 24. Brown Westhead Moore & Co., Cauldonplace about 1850. 25. Cork Edge & Malkin, Burslem 1860–73. 26, 27 and 28. John Dimmock Hanley 1862–1904. 29. Ralph Malkin, Fenton 1863–80. 30. Boote & Co., Burslem 1863–4. 31. James Reeves, Fenton 1870–1930.

10

A SHORT BIBLIOGRAPHY

EARTHENWARE AND STONEWARE

BAINES, J. M., 'Sussex Pottery—1. East Sussex', *Hastings Museum Guide*, No. 17, 1948.

BARNARD, H., *Chats on Wedgwood Ware*, 1924.

BEARD, C. R., *Catalogue of the Collection of Martinware*. Formed by F. J. Nettlefold, 1936.

BLACKER, J. F., *The ABC of English Salt Glaze Stoneware*, 1922.

BOSANKO, W., *Collecting Old Lustre Ware*, 1916.

BURTON, W., *English Earthenware and Stoneware*, 1904.

CAMEHL, A., *The Blue China Book*. New York, 1948.

GRAHAM, J. M., and WEDGWOOD, H. C., *Wedgwood*, New York, 1948.

HAGGAR, R. G., *English Country Pottery*, 1950.

HAYDEN, A., *Chats on English Earthenware*, 1909.

HEMMING, C., 'Sussex Pottery', *Connoisseur*, Vol. XXIV, 1909; *Connoisseur*, Vol. XXXIII, 1912.

HONEY, W. B., *English Pottery and Porcelain*, 1933.

HONEY, W. B., *Wedgwood Ware*, 1948.

JEWITT, L. C., *The Ceramic Art of Great Britain*, 1878.

MOORE, N. H., *The Old China Book*. New York, 1903.

OWEN, H., *Two Centuries of Ceramic Art in Bristol*, 1873.

POUNTNEY, W. J., *The Old Bristol Potteries*, 1920.

READ, H., *Staffordshire Pottery Figures*, 1929.

RHEAD, G. W., *The Earthenware Collector*, 1920.

RHEAD, G. W., and RHEAD, F. A., *Staffordshire Pots and Potters*, 1906.

SHAW, S., *History of the Staffordshire Potteries*, 1829.

THORNE, A., *Pink Lustre Pottery*, 1926.

TURNER, W., *Transfer Printing on Enamel, Porcelain and Pottery*, 1907.

WALTON, J., 'Some Decadent Local Industries—1. Pottery', *Trans. Halifax Antiq. Soc.*, 1938.

WEDGWOOD, J. C., *Staffordshire Pottery and its History*, 1914.

WILLIAMS, S. B., *Antique Blue and White Spode*, 1948.

BIBLIOGRAPHY
PORCELAIN

BARRETT, F. A., *Caughley and Coalport Porcelain*. In preparation.

BINNS, R. W., *A Century of Potting in the City of Worcester*, 1865.

BURTON, W., *A History and Description of English Porcelain*, 1902.

CANNON, T. G., *Old Spode*. N.D.

GILHESPY, F. B., *Crown Derby Porcelain*, 1951.

HASLEM, J., *The Old Derby China Factory*, 1876.

HAYDEN, A., *Spode and his Successors*, 1925.

HURLBUTT, F., *Old Derby Porcelain and its Artist Workmen*, 1925.

HONEY, W. B., *Old English Porcelain*, 1931.

JOHN, W. D., *Nantgarw Porcelain*, 1948.

NANCE, E.M., *The Pottery and Porcelain of Swansea and Nantgarw*, 1943.

WILLIAMS, I. J., *Catalogue of Welsh Porcelain in the National Museum of Wales*, 1932.

WILLIAMS, I. J., *The Nantgarw Pottery and its Products*, 1932.

The *Transactions of the English Ceramic Circle*, prior to 1933 known as The English Porcelain Circle, are a rich source of original information on ceramic topics.

INDEX

INDEX

INDEX

INDEX

Wedgwood, Josiah, Glazes, 39
Wedgwood, Josiah, Lustre, 13
Wedgwood Museum, 13
Wedgwood porcelain, 35, Pl. 9c
Welsh Marches, 6
Wesley, John, (Bust), 17
Westmacot, Sir Richard, R.A., 21
Wilson, Hanley, 14, 15
Wilson, David, Hanley, 18, 19
Wilson, Hanley, 18
Wirksworth, 32
Wood, Enoch, figures, 7
Wood, Enoch, modeller, 17, Pl. 35B

Wood, Enoch, porcelain, 28, 35, 36, Pl. 16B
Wood, Ralph, Factory, 17, 39, Pls. 33A, 33B, 33C
Wood and Caldwell, 14, 15, 18, 24, Pls. 31, 32, 38B, 40A
Woolner, R., R.A., 21
Worcester, 3, 21
Worcester porcelain, 27
Wrotham slipware, 6

Yorkshire, 6, 8, 9, 14, 19
Young, William Weston, 30

PLATES

1. JUG, RED EARTHENWARE, WITH A LEAD GLAZE. SUSSEX
MID-NINETEENTH CENTURY
HEIGHT 11 IN.
See pages 5, 6, 7

2A. HARVEST BARREL, RED EARTHENWARE, BANDED WITH
WHITE SLIP AND LEAD GLAZED. IMPRESSED INSCRIPTION FROM
PRINTER'S TYPE FILLED WITH SLIP DATED 1843. SUSSEX
HEIGHT $6\frac{1}{4}$ IN.
See pages 5, 6, 7
2B. TOBACCO JAR, RED EARTHENWARE DECORATED WITH
IMPRESSED STARS FILLED WITH SLIP UNDER A LEAD GLAZE
INSCRIBED 'W. PAIN 1812'. SUSSEX
HEIGHT, $6\frac{1}{4}$ IN.
See pages 5, 6, 7

3A. CREAM JUG, RED EARTHENWARE, COVERED WITH SLIP WITH
AN INCISED DECORATION UNDER A LEAD GLAZE. ROBERT
FISHLEY FREMINGTON, DATED 1818
HEIGHT, $4\frac{3}{4}$ IN.
See pages 5, 6, 7
3B. CREAM JUG, EARTHENWARE, WITH A LIGHT PURPLISH-
BROWN GLAZE. MARK 'ROCKINGHAM'. J. & W. BRAMELD, SWINTON
EARLY NINETEENTH CENTURY
HEIGHT, 5 IN.
See page 19

4. BARM POT, RED EARTHENWARE DECORATED WHITE SLIP
UNDER A LEAD GLAZE. PENRITH
LATE NINETEENTH CENTURY
HEIGHT 11 IN.
See page 7

5A. TYPICAL COUNTRY WARES: MONEY BOX MARKED 'HALDEN
POTTERY'; HEIGHT, $5\frac{1}{2}$ IN.; MONEY BOX, BURTON IN LONSDALE
HEIGHT, 6 IN.; JUG, SUSSEX; HEIGHT, $5\frac{1}{2}$ IN.
ALL MID-NINETEENTH CENTURY
See pages 5, 6, 7, 8

5B. JUG, PROBABLY BREDE, HEIGHT $6\frac{1}{2}$ IN.; BOWL, SOLID AGATE
WARE, PROBABLY UCKFIELD, DIAM. $7\frac{1}{4}$ IN., BOTH LATE NINE-
TEENTH CENTURY; TWO CREAM JUGS, FREMINGTON, DEVON
ONE DATED 1818
See pages 5, 6, 7, 8

6A. JUG, BROWN SALT-GLAZED STONEWARE. MORTLAKE
(KISHERE'S FACTORY)
EARLY NINETEENTH CENTURY—HEIGHT, $8\frac{1}{2}$ IN.
H. L. Doulton Collection
See page 8

6B. JUG, BROWN SALT-GLAZED STONEWARE. MORTLAKE
(KISHERE'S FACTORY)
EARLY NINETEENTH CENTURY—HEIGHT, $7\frac{1}{4}$ IN.
John Drinkwater Collection
See page 8

6C. JUG, BROWN SALT-GLAZED STONEWARE. LAMBETH
DATED 1818—HEIGHT, 8 IN.
John Drinkwater Collection
See page 8

7A. HOUND, DOG AND LION, BROWN SALT-GLAZED STONEWARE
PROBABLY CHESTERFIELD
ABOUT 1825
GREATEST HEIGHT, $3\frac{3}{4}$ IN.
John Drinkwater Collection. See page 8
7B. TOBY-JUG, BROWN SALT-GLAZED STONEWARE. BRAMPTON
EARLY NINETEENTH CENTURY
HEIGHT $10\frac{1}{4}$ IN.
John Drinkwater Collection. See page 8

8A & B. SAUCER AND TEAPOT, PORCELAIN, PAINTED IN RED &
BROWN ENAMEL COLOURS AND GILT. STOKE-ON-TRENT
(MINTON FACTORY). ABOUT 1820
DIAM. $5\frac{3}{8}$ IN. AND HEIGHT 6 IN. RESPECTIVELY
See page 31
8C. TEAPOT, PORCELAIN, PAINTED IN UNDERGLAZE BLUE AND GILT
MARK, 'RALPH CLOWES NEWHALL FECIT', INCISED. SHELTON
(NEW HALL FACTORY); ABOUT 1800. HEIGHT, 6 IN.
Victoria and Albert Museum
See page 32

9A. TEA-CUP AND SAUCER, PORCELAIN, PAINTED IN 'SILVER'
LUSTRE AND RED. SHELTON (NEW HALL TYPE)
ABOUT 1810–20. HEIGHT OF CUP, 2 IN.
Victoria and Albert Museum. See page 32
9B. JUG, PORCELAIN, PAINTED IN ENAMEL COLOURS BY FIDELE
DUVIVIER, (NEW HALL FACTORY). ABOUT 1800. HEIGHT, $5\frac{1}{2}$ IN.
See page 32
9C. COFFEE CAN AND SAUCER, PORCELAIN, DECORATED WITH
BOTANICAL PRINTS WASHED OVER IN ENAMEL COLOURS. MARK
'WEDGWOOD' IN RED
ABOUT 1812. HEIGHT OF CAN, $2\frac{1}{2}$ IN. *See page* 35.

10A. TEA-CUP AND SAUCER, PORCELAIN, PAINTED IN COLOURS
MARK 'NEW HALL' WITHIN A DOUBLE CIRCLE, PRINTED IN RED.
SHELTON (NEW HALL FACTORY)
ABOUT 1810–15. HEIGHT OF CUP, $2\frac{1}{4}$ IN.
Victoria and Albert Museum. See page 32

10B. CUP AND SAUCER, PORCELAIN, PAINTED IN PINK LUSTRE
AND COLOURS. PROBABLY SHELTON (NEW HALL FACTORY)
ABOUT 1820. HEIGHT OF CUP, $2\frac{1}{4}$ IN.
Victoria and Albert Museum. See page 32

10C. DISH, PORCELAIN, MOULDED IN RELIEF ON A BLUE
GROUND AND PAINTED IN COLOURS. MARK 'NEW HALL' WITHIN
A DOUBLE CIRCLE PRINTED IN BLACK. SHELTON (NEW HALL
FACTORY)
ABOUT 1815. LENGTH, $7\frac{3}{4}$ IN.
See page 32

11A. DISH, PORCELAIN, PAINTED IN SEPIA WITHIN A PURPLE
AND GILT BORDER. MARK 'M. MASON'. LANE END
ABOUT 1800. 8 IN SQUARE
See page 35

11B. PLATE, WHITE EARTHENWARE, PAINTED IN COLOURS
MARK 'SPODE' IMPRESSED. STOKE-ON-TRENT (SPODE FACTORY)
EARLY NINETEENTH CENTURY
DIAM. $8\frac{3}{4}$ IN.
Victoria and Albert Museum
See page 12

12. JUG, WHITE EARTHENWARE, PAINTED IN BLUE, ORANGE,
GREEN, YELLOW AND BROWN IN PEASANT STYLE AND DATED
1814. TUNSTALL (ADAMS FACTORY, GREENFIELDS)
HEIGHT, $6\frac{1}{2}$ IN.
See page 9

13A. BOTTLE, EARTHENWARE, PAINTED IN BLUE, YELLOW AND
BROWN IN PEASANT STYLE. STAFFORDSHIRE
ABOUT 1810. HEIGHT, $5\frac{1}{2}$ IN.
Leicester Museum and Art Gallery
See page 9
13B. HARVEST JUG, EARTHENWARE PAINTED IN BLUE, RED,
BROWN AND GREEN IN PEASANT STYLE. STAFFORDSHIRE
ABOUT 1810. HEIGHT 6 IN.
See page 9

14. JUG, EARTHENWARE, PAINTED IN ORANGE, YELLOW AND
BLUE. STAFFORDSHIRE
EARLY NINETEENTH CENTURY
HEIGHT, $5\frac{3}{4}$ IN.
Victoria and Albert Museum
See page 13

15. JUG, EARTHENWARE, PAINTED IN COLOURS. PROBABLY LEEDS
EARLY NINETEENTH CENTURY
HEIGHT, $5\frac{5}{8}$ IN.
Victoria and Albert Museum
See page 12

16A. DISH, EARTHENWARE, PAINTED IN BLACK; DARK-GREEN
AND LUSTRE BORDER. MARK 'HARTLEY GREENS & CO. LEEDS
POTTERY'. ABOUT 1820
GREATEST WIDTH $10\frac{1}{8}$ IN.
Victoria and Albert Museum
See page 12
16B. BULB-POT, PORCELAIN, PAINTED IN COLOURS AND GILT.
MARK W (* * *) BURSLEM (ENOCH WOOD & SONS FACTORY)
ABOUT 1820. HEIGHT, 6 IN.
See page 36

17A. DISH, EARTHENWARE, PAINTED IN WHITE, BROWN AND
BLACK ON A DRAB GROUND. MARK 'LAKIN' IMPRESSED
STOKE-ON-TRENT (THOMAS LAKIN'S FACTORY)
EARLY NINETEENTH CENTURY
GREATEST WIDTH, $8\frac{1}{8}$ IN.
Victoria and Albert Museum
See page 13

17B. TEAPOT, EARTHENWARE, PAINTED ON A SALMON-PINK
GROUND IN SEPIA AND GILT. MARK 'DAVENPORT' IMPRESSED
LONGPORT. ABOUT 1815
HEIGHT, $3\frac{1}{2}$ IN.
See page 13

18A. PLATE, EARTHENWARE, WITH A BLUE GROUND DECORATED
WITH RESERVE PRINTS IN BLACK OF KNYPERSLEY, STAFFS.
MARK 'SPODE' IMPRESSED AND DATED 1832
DIAM. 10 IN.
See page 26
18B. PLATE, PORCELAIN, PRINTED IN GOLD; BLUE AND GOLD
PAINTED BORDER. MARK, 'WARBURTON'S PATENT' UNDER A
CROWN, IN RED. PROBABLY SHELTON (NEW HALL FACTORY)
ABOUT 1810. DIAM. 8¾ IN.
Victoria and Albert Museum
See page 32

19A. SOUP-PLATE, EARTHENWARE, TRANSFER PRINTED IN
STIPPLE WITH A PORTRAIT OF NELSON. MARK 'HERCULANEUM'
IMPRESSED. LIVERPOOL, 1805
DIAM. $9\frac{7}{8}$ IN.
See page 36
19B. JUG, PORCELAIN, STIPPLE PRINTED IN PURPLE AND
WASHED OVER IN ENAMEL COLOURS. BLUE ENAMEL AND GILT
BORDER. NEW HALL FACTORY
ABOUT 1810. HEIGHT, $5\frac{1}{2}$ IN.
See page 32

20A. JUG, WHITE EARTHENWARE DECORATED WITH A 'SILVER'
RESIST LUSTRE PATTERN. STAFFORDSHIRE
EARLY NINETEENTH CENTURY. HEIGHT, $4\frac{1}{2}$ IN.
20B. COFFEE POT, WHITE EARTHENWARE PAINTED IN SILVER
LUSTRE AND ENAMELLED RED AND GREEN. STOKE-ON-TRENT
(PROBABLY W. ADAMS FACTORY). ABOUT 1810. HEIGHT, $5\frac{1}{2}$ IN.
20C. JUG, EARTHENWARE, DECORATED IN 'SILVER' RESIST
LUSTRE AND PAINTED WITH BIRDS IN PANELS. STAFFORDSHIRE
EARLY NINETEENTH CENTURY. HEIGHT, $4\frac{3}{8}$ IN.
20D. GOBLET, EARTHENWARE, DECORATED IN PINK LUSTRE
AND PAINTED IN RED AND GREEN ENAMELS. PROBABLY, SWANSEA
EARLY NINETEENTH CENTURY. HEIGHT, $4\frac{5}{8}$ IN.
20E. CUP AND SAUCER, PORCELAIN, DECORATED IN PINK LUSTRE
AND RED ENAMEL. PROBABLY, MINTON EARLY NINETEENTH
CENTURY. HEIGHT OF CUP, $2\frac{1}{4}$ IN
20F. JUG, EARTHENWARE, DECORATED IN PINK LUSTRE.
STAFFORDSHIRE; EARLY NINETEENTH CENTURY. HEIGHT $4\frac{1}{2}$ IN.
See pages 13, 14, 15

21A. PAIR OF VASES, BUFF EARTHENWARE, PRINTED WITH A
CONTINUOUS VIEW IN BLACK AND LUSTRED. PROBABLY WILSON,
HANLEY; EARLY NINETEENTH CENTURY. HEIGHT, $7\frac{1}{8}$ IN.
21B. PLATE, WHITE EARTHENWARE, DECORATED IN 'SILVER'
RESIST LUSTRE. STAFFORDSHIRE; EARLY NINETEENTH CENTURY
DIAM. $7\frac{1}{2}$ IN.
21C. JUG, WHITE EARTHENWARE, DECORATED IN 'SILVER'
RESIST LUSTRE. STAFFORDSHIRE; MID-LATE NINETEENTH
CENTURY. HEIGHT, $4\frac{1}{8}$ IN.
21D. BEAKER, WHITE EARTHENWARE, PAINTED IN 'SILVER'
LUSTRE. STAFFORDSHIRE; EARLY NINETEENTH CENTURY.
HEIGHT, $5\frac{1}{4}$ IN.
21E. JUG, WHITE EARTHENWARE, DECORATED IN 'SILVER'
RESIST LUSTRE. STAFFORDSHIRE; EARLY NINETEENTH CENTURY.
HEIGHT, $4\frac{1}{2}$ IN. *See pages* 13, 14, 15

22. JUG, EARTHENWARE, DECORATED IN 'SILVER' LUSTRE
STAFFORDSHIRE
EARLY NINETEENTH CENTURY
HEIGHT, $5\frac{1}{2}$ IN.
Victoria and Albert Museum
See page 14

23. JUG, EARTHENWARE, DECORATED IN PINK LUSTRE
STAFFORDSHIRE
EARLY NINETEENTH CENTURY
HEIGHT, $5\frac{1}{2}$ IN.
Victoria and Albert Museum
See page 14

24A & B. TWO SAUCERS, PORCELAIN, PAINTED IN PINK LUSTRE
STAFFORDSHIRE
EARLY NINETEENTH CENTURY
DIAM. $5\frac{1}{2}$ IN.
24C. DISH, EARTHENWARE, WITH AN ELABORATE 'SILVER'
RESIST LUSTRE PATTERN. MARK 'ROGERS' IMPRESSED. LONGPORT
(J. J. ROGERS FACTORY)
ABOUT 1810
LENGTH, 17 IN.
See page 14

25A. JUG, PORCELAIN, PAINTED IN RED AND BLUE ENAMEL
COLOURS AND BANDED IN PINK LUSTRE. STAFFORDSHIRE
PROBABLY NEW HALL FACTORY, EARLY NINETEENTH CENTURY
HEIGHT, 4 IN.

25B. JUG, EARTHENWARE, DECORATED IN 'SILVER' RESIST
LUSTRE ON A CANARY YELLOW GROUND. STAFFORDSHIRE
EARLY NINETEENTH CENTURY. HEIGHT, $4\frac{3}{4}$ IN.

25C. MUG, EARTHENWARE, WITH A BLACK PRINTED VIEW ON
A CANARY YELLOW GROUND OUTLINED IN 'SILVER' LUSTRE
STAFFORDSHIRE; EARLY NINETEENTH CENTURY. HEIGHT, $3\frac{1}{4}$ IN.

25D. JUG, EARTHENWARE, PAINTED IN 'SILVER' LUSTRE AND
RED ENAMEL ON A CANARY YELLOW GROUND. STAFFORDSHIRE
EARLY NINETEENTH CENTURY. HEIGHT, $5\frac{3}{4}$ IN.

See page 14, 15

26A. MUG, EARTHENWARE (WICKER HANDLE) DECORATED
WITH BANDS OF GROUND LAID COLOURS—ORANGE, BLUE, GREEN
AND DARK BROWN. MOCHA WARE MADE BY ADAMS, TUNSTALL
ABOUT 1800. HEIGHT, $4\frac{1}{4}$ IN.
See pages 10, 11

26B. BASIN, EARTHENWARE, BANDED IN COLOURS AND
DECORATED IN BROWN AND WHITE SLIP. STAFFORDSHIRE
ABOUT 1810 HEIGHT, $2\frac{7}{8}$ IN.
See pages 9, 10

27. JUG, EARTHENWARE, BANDED IN GREY AND BLUE SLIP
AND DECORATED WITH FINGER TRAILING IN BROWN, ORANGE
AND BLUE. MARK 'COPELAND & GARRETT' STOKE
ABOUT 1835. HEIGHT, $5\frac{1}{2}$ IN.
See pages 9, 10

28A. TEAPOT, UNGLAZED WHITE PORCELAIN, MOULDED AND
LINED IN BLUE ENAMEL. MARK 'HEATH & SON' IMPRESSED
TUNSTALL; ABOUT 1820. HEIGHT, $5\frac{1}{2}$ IN.
28B. TEAPOT, GLAZED PORCELAIN WITH MOULDED DECORATION
OUTLINED IN BLUE ENAMEL AND A PAINTED LANDSCAPE
OUTLINED IN CHOCOLATE ENAMEL. CASTLEFORD; EARLY
NINETEENTH CENTURY. HEIGHT, 5 IN.
See pages 15, 16
28C. CREAM JUG, BONE-CHINA PORCELAIN, MOULDED AND
PAINTED IN BLUE, RED, GREEN AND GILT. MARK 'RILEY 1823'
BURSLEM. HEIGHT, $4\frac{1}{2}$ IN.
See page 35

29. MANTELPIECE, IRONSTONE CHINA WITH MOULDED
DECORATION PAINTED IN COLOURS ON A YELLOW GROUND.
FROM CHARLES MASON'S HOUSE, DUKE ST., FENTON. C. & J.
MASON'S FACTORY. ABOUT 1815
HEIGHT, 3 FT. 8 IN.
See page 16

30A. BUST OF PRIOR, EARTHENWARE PAINTED IN BROWN AND
PINK ENAMELS WITH A 'SILVER' LUSTRE PLINTH. ENOCH WOOD
BURSLEM; EARLY NINETEENTH CENTURY. HEIGHT, 8 IN.
See page 17
30B. BUST OF ENOCH WOOD BY HIMSELF. EARTHENWARE
PAINTED BLACK AND LIGHTLY FIRED. THE REVERSE BEARS AN
IMPORTANT INSCRIPTION DATED 1821. HEIGHT, 23 IN.
See page 17

31. GROUP: THE VIRGIN AND CHILD, EARTHENWARE, PAINTED
IN ENAMEL COLOURS. BURSLEM (PROBABLY, WOOD &
CALDWELL'S FACTORY)
EARLY NINETEENTH CENTURY
HEIGHT 13⅝ IN.
See page 18

32. FIGURE OF FORTITUDE. EARTHENWARE DECORATED IN PALE
ENAMEL COLOURS, PINK PREDOMINATING, WITH A MARBLED
PLINTH. ENOCH WOOD, BURSLEM
EARLY NINETEENTH CENTURY
HEIGHT, $21\frac{1}{2}$ IN.
See pages 17, 18

33A. FIGURE GROUP, EARTHENWARE, PAINTED IN ENAMEL
COLOURS. A LATE PRODUCTION OF THE R. WOOD FACTORY
BURSLEM; ABOUT 1800. HEIGHT, $10\frac{1}{2}$ IN.

33B. FIGURE, EARTHENWARE, DECORATED IN COLOURS
UNDERGLAZE. EXCAVATED IN BURSLEM MARKET PLACE 1938
STAFFORDSHIRE; EARLY NINETEENTH CENTURY. HEIGHT, 61 IN.

33C. FIGURE OF ELIJAH, EARTHENWARE, DECORATED IN COLOURS
UNDERGLAZE. EXCAVATED IN BURSLEM MARKET PLACE 1938
PROBABLY A LATE PRODUCTION OF THE R. WOOD FACTORY
ABOUT 1800. HEIGHT, 9 IN.

See page 17

34A. FIGURE GROUP, EARTHENWARE PAINTED IN ENAMEL
COLOURS. STAFFORDSHIRE; ABOUT 1820. HEIGHT, 9¾ IN.
See page 17
34B. BULL BAITING GROUP, EARTHENWARE PAINTED IN ENAMEL
COLOURS. INSCRIBED 'BULL BEATING' AND 'NOW CAPTIN LAD'
BURSLEM (OBADIAH SHERRATT FACTORY); ABOUT 1830
HEIGHT, 10 IN.
See page 18

55A. GROUP OF THE FLIGHT INTO EGYPT, EARTHENWARE
PAINTED IN ENAMEL COLOURS. BURSLEM (WALTON FACTORY)
ABOUT 1825–30. HEIGHT, 10 IN.
See page 17

55B. FIGURE OF LUCRETIA, EARTHENWARE, PAINTED IN ENAMEL
COLOURS. BURSLEM (ENOCH WOOD FACTORY); ABOUT 1820
LENGTH, $11\frac{3}{4}$ IN.
Victoria and Albert Museum
See pages 17, 18

36. FIGURE OF THE SECOND DUKE OF CAMBRIDGE, EARTHEN-
WARE, PAINTED IN COLOURS. LONGTON (SAMPSON SMITH
FACTORY); ABOUT 1840–50. HEIGHT, $14\frac{1}{2}$ IN.
Victoria and Albert Museum
See page 19

37A. FIGURE, EARTHENWARE, DECORATED IN DEEP UNDER-
GLAZE BLUE AND ENAMEL COLOURS AND GILT. LONGTON
(SAMPSON SMITH FACTORY); MID-NINETEENTH CENTURY
HEIGHT, 16 IN.
See page 19

37B. TWO FIGURES, PORCELAIN, PAINTED IN ENAMEL COLOURS.
INSCRIBED 'SCHOOLMASTER' AND 'PUPIL'. SHELTON (BROWN-
WESTHEAD MOORE FACTORY); ABOUT 1865. HEIGHT, $8\frac{1}{4}$ IN.
AND $7\frac{1}{2}$ IN.
See page 35

38A. PLATE, EARTHENWARE, PRINTED IN UNDERGLAZE BLUE
WITH A WILLOW PATTERN AND INSCRIBED 'THOMASINE WILLEY
1818'. PROBABLY STAFFORDSHIRE. DIAM. $8\frac{5}{8}$ IN.
See pages 23, 24
38B. PLATE, EARTHENWARE, PRINTED IN UNDERGLAZE BLUE
WITH A VIEW OF THE COURT-HOUSE, BOSTON, U.S.A. MARK
'WOOD & CALDWELL' IMPRESSED. BURSLEM; ABOUT 1818
DIAM., $9\frac{1}{2}$ IN.
See page 24

39A. PLATE, EARTHENWARE, PRINTED IN UNDERGLAZE BLUE MARK 'WATERWORKS PHILADELPHIA RSW'. COBRIDGE (RALPH STEVENSON & WILLIAMS FACTORY); ABOUT 1818. DIAM. 10 IN.
39B. PLATE, EARTHENWARE, PRINTED IN DARK BLUE UNDERGLAZE. MARK 'DR. SYNTAX AND THE BEES'. 'CLEWS. WARRANTED STAFFORDSHIRE' IMPRESSED. COBRIDGE ABOUT 1820. DIAM., 10 IN.

See page 24

40A. PLATE, EARTHENWARE, PRINTED IN UNDERGLAZE BLUE
MARK 'E. WOOD & SONS, BURSLEM WARRANTED', IMPRESSED
ABOUT 1835. DIAM., $10\frac{1}{8}$ IN.
Victoria and Albert Museum
40B. DISH, EARTHENWARE, PRINTED IN UNDERGLAZE BLUE
MARK 'WEDGWOOD' IMPRESSED; ABOUT 1820. $9\frac{1}{4}$ IN. SQ.
See page 24

41A. DISH, EARTHENWARE, PRINTED IN DARK BLUE UNDER-
GLAZE. MARK 'HANOVER TERRACE, REGENT'S PARK'. 'ADAMS
WARRANTED STAFFORDSHIRE' IMPRESSED; ABOUT 1815.
LENGTH, $8\frac{1}{4}$ IN.
41B. PLATE, EARTHENWARE, PRINTED IN UNDERGLAZE BLUE
MARK 'FOUNTAINS ABBEY' AND 'CLEWS WARRANTED STAFFORDSHIRE'
IMPRESSED; COBRIDGE; ABOUT 1830. DIAM., 10 IN.
See page 24

42. JUG, EARTHENWARE, PRINTED IN UNDERGLAZE BLUE
FENTON (BOURNE, BAKER & BOURNE'S FACTORY); ABOUT 1630
HEIGHT, $27\frac{3}{4}$ IN.
Victoria and Albert Museum
See page 24

43. DISH, EARTHENWARE PRINTED IN UNDERGLAZE BLUE
MARK 'WEDGWOOD' IMPRESSED
ABOUT 1830. LENGTH 20⅝IN.
Victoria and Albert Museum
See page 24

44A. PLATE, CANEWARE, PRINTED IN UNDERGLAZE BLACK
MARK 'NEAR FISH KILL HUDSON RIVER' COBRIDGE (JAMES
CLEWS FACTORY); ABOUT 1825. DIAM., 10 IN.
See page 24

44B. PLATE, EARTHENWARE, PRINTED IN GREEN. MARK
'A VIEW IN VENICE'. SHELTON (JOHN RIDGWAY); 1830–35.
DIAM., 10 IN.
See page 23

45A. PLATE, EARTHENWARE, PRINTED IN BROWN. MARK 'APPLE
BLOSSOM W.R.S. & CO.' IMPRESSED. HANLEY (W. RIDGWAY &
SON CHURCH WORKS); ABOUT 1840. LENGTH, 11 IN.
45B. PLATE, EARTHENWARE, PRINTED IN YELLOW AND BLACK
MARK OF WILLIAM RIDGWAY & CO. HANLEY; ABOUT 1840.
DIAM., $9\frac{1}{4}$ IN.
Victoria and Albert Museum

See page 25

46A. COFFEE-CUP AND SAUCER, PORCELAIN PAINTED IN COLOURS
AND GILT. STOKE-ON-TRENT (MINTON FACTORY); ABOUT 1820
HEIGHT OF CUP, $2\frac{1}{2}$ IN.
Victoria and Albert Museum
See page 31
46B. PLATE, PORCELAIN, PAINTED IN RED, DARK BLUE AND
GILT. MARK 'CHAMBERLAIN WORCESTER' IN RED; EARLY
NINETEENTH CENTURY
See page 29

47. VASE, PORCELAIN, PAINTED IN COLOURS AND GILT. MARK
'CHAMBERLAINS WOR. NO. 276', WRITTEN IN RED. WORCESTER
EARLY NINETEENTH CENTURY
HEIGHT, $19\frac{1}{4}$ IN.
Victoria and Albert Museum
See page 29

48A. CREAM JUG, PORCELAIN, PAINTED IN DARK BLUE AND
GILT. SHELTON (NEW HALL FACTORY); ABOUT 1820
HEIGHT, $3\frac{1}{4}$ IN.
See page 31
48B. CUP AND SAUCER, PORCELAIN, PAINTED IN BLUE, RED AND
GREEN ENAMELS AND GILT. MARK CROSSED LS. STOKE-ON-
TRENT (THOMAS MINTON); ABOUT 1820–25
HEIGHT OF CUP, $2\frac{3}{8}$ IN.
See page 29
48C. TEA-CUP AND SAUCER, PORCELAIN, PAINTED IN COLOURS
AND GILT. STOKE-ON-TRENT (SPODE); ABOUT 1820
HEIGHT OF CUP, $2\frac{1}{4}$ IN.
Victoria and Albert Museum
See page 26

49. TUREEN AND STAND, IRONSTONE CHINA, MOULDED
DECORATION PAINTED OVER IN LIGHT AND DARK BLUE, RED,
PINK AND GREEN. MARK 'STONE CHINA NO. 6' PROBABLY SPODE
EARLY NINETEENTH CENTURY
HEIGHT, 12 IN.
See pages 16, 17

50. VASE, PORCELAIN, PAINTED WITH A CONTINUOUS VIEW AND
GILT. MARK 'BLOOR DERBY' IN RED
ABOUT 1830
HEIGHT, 11 IN.
See pages 27, 28

51. VASE, PORCELAIN, PAINTED IN COLOURS. THE GILDING IS
ON A DARK BLUE GROUND. PROBABLY DERBY
EARLY NINETEENTH CENTURY
HEIGHT, 12 IN.
See pages 27, 28

52. VASE, PORCELAIN, PAINTED IN COLOURS AND GILT, OLIVE-
GREEN GROUND. SWINTON (ROCKINGHAM WORKS)
ABOUT 1825
HEIGHT, 13 IN.
Victoria and Albert Museum
See page 33

55. VASE, PORCELAIN, PAINTED IN COLOURS AND GILT. DERBY
ABOUT 1820
HEIGHT, 15¾ IN.
Victoria and Albert Museum
See pages 27, 28

54A & B. PAIR OF SPILL-VASES, PORCELAIN, PAINTED IN COLOURS
AND GILT BY THOMAS BAXTER. SWANSEA
ABOUT 1816. HEIGHT, 5 IN.
Victoria and Albert Museum
54C. PLATE, PORCELAIN, PAINTED IN COLOURS AND GILT, AND
SIGNED BY THOMAS BAXTER. WORCESTER; DATED 1808.
DIAM., $9\frac{3}{8}$ IN.
Victoria and Albert Museum
See page 29

55A. BEAKER, PORCELAIN, PAINTED IN COLOURS AND GILT BY
THOMAS BAXTER. MARK 'CHAMBERLAINS WORCESTER' WRITTEN
IN GOLD; ABOUT 1820. HEIGHT, $3\frac{3}{8}$ IN.
Victoria and Albert Museum. See page 29
55B. SPILL VASE, PORCELAIN, PAINTED IN COLOURS AND GILT
MARK CROSSED LS. STOKE-ON-TRENT (THOMAS MINTON); ABOUT
1820. HEIGHT, $4\frac{1}{2}$ IN. *See page* 31
55C. BEAKER, PORCELAIN, PAINTED IN SEPIA BY JAMES
PENNINGTON, AND GILT. MARK 'FLIGHT & BARR WORR'
ABOUT 1810. HEIGHT, $3\frac{3}{4}$ IN. *See page* 29
55D. CACHE-POT AND STAND, PORCELAIN, PAINTED IN RESERVE
PANELS ON YELLOW GROUND BY JOHN BREWER. MARK D UNDER
A CROWN WITH CROSSED BATONS. DERBY; ABOUT 1820
HEIGHT, $4\frac{1}{2}$ IN. *See page* 27

56. PLATE, PORCELAIN, PAINTED IN COLOURS AND GILT
MARK 'ACONITE. SPODE' IN PURPLE
ABOUT 1810
DIAM., $6\frac{1}{2}$ IN
See page 27

57. PLATE, PORCELAIN, PAINTED IN COLOURS AND GILT WITH
BIRDS COPIED FROM PLATES IN 'THE NATURAL HISTORY OF
BRITISH BIRDS', BY E. DONOVAN, LONDON, 1794. MARK 'SPODE'
WRITTEN IN RED. STOKE-ON-TRENT (SPODE FACTORY)
ABOUT 1815
DIAM., $9\frac{3}{4}$ IN.
Victoria and Albert Museum
See page 27

58A. CUP AND SAUCER, PORCELAIN, PAINTED IN COLOURS BY
THOMAS STEELE, AND GILT MARK, AN ANCHOR LABELLED
'DAVENPORT'; ABOUT 1820–25. HEIGHT OF CUP, $2\frac{1}{4}$ IN.
See page 34
58B. PLATE, PORCELAIN, PAINTED IN COLOURS AND GILT
MARK 'NANT-GARW C.W.' IMPRESSED. 1813–1820. DIAM. $9\frac{3}{4}$ IN.
Victoria and Albert Museum
See pages 29, 30

59A. INKSTAND, PORCELAIN, PAINTED IN COLOURS
AND GILT. NANTGARW. 1813–20. HEIGHT, $3\frac{3}{4}$ IN. LENGTH, $7\frac{1}{8}$ IN.
National Museum of Wales, Cardiff
See pages 29, 30

59B. VASE, PORCELAIN, PAINTED IN COLOURS BY W. POLLARD
AND GILT. MARK 'POLLARD CAMARTHEN' IN RED SCRIPT
?SWANSEA, ABOUT 1815. HEIGHT, $7\frac{3}{4}$ IN.
National Museum of Wales, Cardiff
See page 31

60A. BEAKER, PORCELAIN, PAINTED IN RESERVE ON A BLUE
GROUND AND GILT. MARK 'NANTGARW' PRINTED IN RED
1813–20. HEIGHT, $5\frac{1}{4}$ IN.
See pages 29, 30

60B. PLATE, PORCELAIN, PAINTED IN COLOURS AND GILT BY
THOMAS BAXTER. MARK 'SWANSEA' WRITTEN IN RED. 1816
DIAM., $8\frac{1}{2}$ IN.
Victoria and Albert Museum
See page 29

61A. SUGAR-BOWL, PORCELAIN, PAINTED IN COLOURS AND GILT
TURQUOISE-BLUE GROUND. MARK 'SWANSEA' PRINTED IN RED
ABOUT 1814–17. HEIGHT, $4\frac{5}{8}$ IN.
Victoria and Albert Museum
See page 30
61B. PLATE, PORCELAIN, PAINTED IN COLOURS AND GILT
CREAM GROUND. MARK 'SPODE FELSPAR PORCELAIN' PRINTED
IN PURPLE. STOKE-ON-TRENT (SPODE); ABOUT 1830.
DIAM. 9 IN.
Victoria and Albert Museum. See page 26

62A. MUG, PORCELAIN, PAINTED IN COLOURS AND GILT
PROBABLY COALPORT; ABOUT 1830. HEIGHT, $4\frac{1}{4}$ IN.
Victoria and Albert Museum
See page 33

62B. PUNCH-BOWL, PORCELAIN, PAINTED IN ORANGE-RED ON A
GILT GROUND. MARK 'D' UNDER A CROWN, WITH CROSSED
BATONS AND SIX DOTS, IN RED. DERBY; ABOUT 1820
DIAM. $10\frac{3}{4}$ IN.
Victoria and Albert Museum
See page 27

63A. VASE, PORCELAIN, WITH APPLIED FLOWERS AND TWIG
HANDLES. PAINTED IN COLOURS. MARK, CROSSED SWORDS
COALPORT; ABOUT 1840. HEIGHT, $7\frac{3}{4}$ IN.
Fitzwilliam Museum, Cambridge
63B. TRAY WITH PAIR OF TOILET-POTS, PORCELAIN, PAINTED IN
COLOURS. COALPORT; ABOUT 1830. GREATEST WIDTH OF TRAY,
$12\frac{1}{2}$ IN. *Victoria and Albert Museum*
See page 33

64A. COFFEE POT, EARTHENWARE, DECORATED WITH POLY-
CHROME PRINTS UNDERGLAZE IN RESERVE ON A GREEN
GROUND. FENTON (F. & R. PRATT & CO. FACTORY); ABOUT
1850. HEIGHT, 7 IN.
See page 23

64B. PLATE, EARTHENWARE, DECORATED IN GOLD ON A BUFF
GROUND. THE CENTRE PAINTED IN COLOURS. HANLEY (MEIGH
OLD HALL FACTORY) MARK 'OPAQUE PORCELAIN' ABOUT 1850
DIAM. $9\frac{1}{2}$ IN.
See page 37

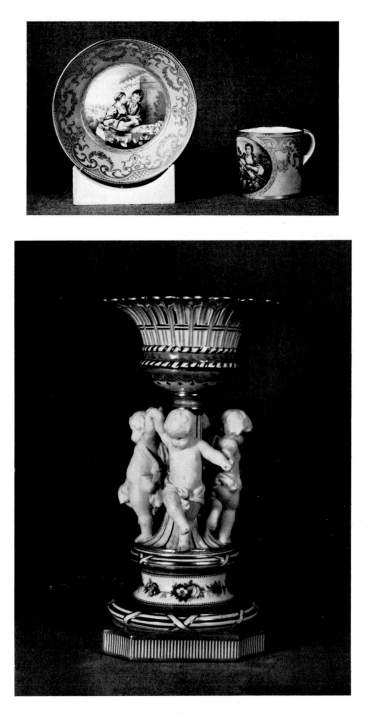

65A. COFFEE CAN AND SAUCER, PORCELAIN, PAINTED IN COLOURS
ON A ROSE PINK GROUND WITH TOOLED GILDING. MARK
'C B D' COALPORT; ABOUT 1850. HEIGHT OF CAN, $2\frac{3}{4}$ IN.
See page 33

65B. TAZZA, PORCELAIN, WITH BISQUE CUPIDS PAINTED IN
COLOURS ON A TURQUOISE GROUND. STOKE-ON-TRENT (MINTON
FACTORY); ABOUT 1850. HEIGHT, 10 IN.
See page 39

66. TRAY, PORCELAIN, DECORATED EN CAMAÏEU ON A PINK
GROUND AND GILT WITH FESTOONS OF FLOWERS AND A CENTRE
PANEL IN COLOURS. STOKE-ON-TRENT (MINTON FACTORY)
ABOUT 1860
LENGTH, $12\frac{1}{4}$ IN.
See page 38

67. VASE AND STAND, PORCELAIN, PAINTED WITH PANELS OF
FLOWERS AND GILDING ON A TURQUOISE GROUND. MARK
'MINTON' IMPRESSED AND PRINTED
ABOUT 1865
HEIGHT, 7½ IN.
See page 38

68. VASE, PORCELAIN, PAINTED WITH FLOWER SPRAYS IN
RESERVE ON A GREEN GROUND AND GILT. MARK 'C B D' IN
BLUE, COALPORT; ABOUT 1850. HEIGHT, 16 IN.
Nottingham Castle Museum

See page 33

69. VASE AND COVER, PORCELAIN, PAINTED IN COLOURS AND
GILT. MARK 'DAVENPORT' AND AN ANCHOR; ABOUT 1850
HEIGHT, 19 IN.
Nottingham Castle Museum
See page 34

70. PLAQUE, PORCELAIN, PAINTED IN COLOURS BY THOMAS
STEELE SIGNED AND DATED 1846. DERBY OR LONGPORT
(DAVENPORT FACTORY); 14 IN. × 10 IN.
See page 34

71. LITHOPHANE PANEL OF WHITE PORCELAIN IMPRESSED WITH
A REPRODUCTION OF AN OLD MASTER PAINTING
STOKE-ON-TRENT (COPELAND FACTORY)
LATE NINETEENTH CENTURY
HEIGHT, $12\frac{1}{2}$ IN.
See page 43

72. PLAQUE, PORCELAIN, PAINTED IN WHITE SHADED WITH
BLUE ON A DARK BLUE GROUND. MARK 'THE SIREN BY THOS.
JNO. BOTT, WORCESTER 1883'
DIAM., 6 IN.
See page 41

73. TRAY, PORCELAIN, PAINTED IN COLOURS AND SIGNED BY
DAN LUCAS. STOKE-ON-TRENT (COPELAND FACTORY)
ABOUT 1860–70
LENGTH, $14\frac{1}{2}$ IN.
See page 27

74. PARIAN BUST OF THE PRINCE CONSORT. MARK 'W. THEED
SC. COPELAND'
ABOUT 1850
HEIGHT, 14 IN.
Collection of Miss Fanny Andrews
See page 21

75. PARIAN BUST OF THE FIRST DUKE OF WELLINGTON
INSCRIBED 'C. TOFT FECIT 1853'
STOKE-ON-TRENT (MINTON FACTORY)
HEIGHT, $9\frac{1}{2}$ IN.
See page 21

76. PARIAN GROUP IMPRESSED 'VISION OF THE RED CROSSE
KNIGHT' AND MARKED 'JOSEPH PITTS 1851'
HEIGHT, $18\frac{1}{4}$ IN.
Collection of Dr. Albert Baillie, K.C.V.O., D.D.
See page 22

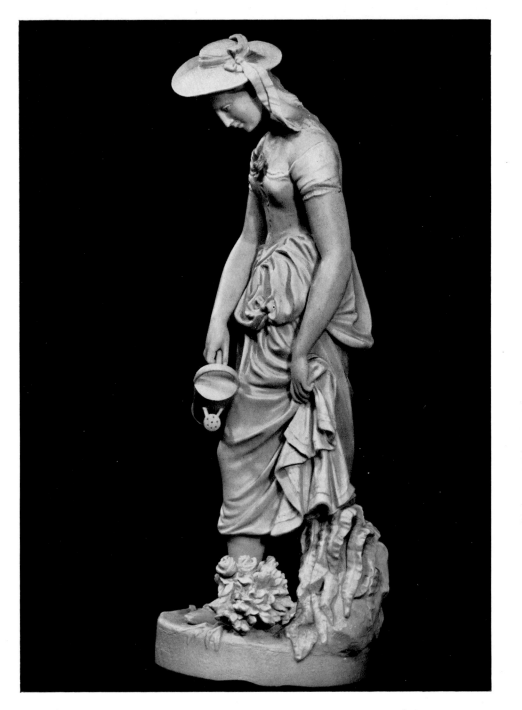

77. PARIAN GROUP OF CHRISTINA LINNAEUS. MARK 'G. HALSE
SC. COPELAND'
ABOUT 1850
HEIGHT, 23 IN.
Collection of Miss Fanny Andrews
See page 22

78. PARIAN FIGURE OF FANNY ELSSLER. STAFFORDSHIRE
PERHAPS COPELAND
ABOUT 1850
HEIGHT, 14 IN.
See page 22

79. FIGURE IN FIRED CLAY OF SPRING. INSCRIBED 'A CARRIER
BELLEUSE'. COBRIDGE (W. BROWNFIELD & SONS FACTORY)
ABOUT 1880
HEIGHT, 16 IN.
See page 21

80. VASE, EARTHENWARE, PAINTED IN ENAMEL COLOURS BY
EMILE LESSORE. MARK 'WEDGWOOD' IMPRESSED
ABOUT 1870
HEIGHT, 5 IN.
See page 38

81. PLATE, EARTHENWARE, MOULDED IN RELIEF WITH A
DESIGN BY LEONARD ABINGTON AND GLAZED GREEN. HANLEY
(RIDGWAY & ABINGTON FACTORY)
ABOUT 1865
DIAM., $8\frac{3}{8}$ IN.
See page 39

82A. FIGURE, CANEWARE, DECORATED WITH 'MAJOLICA' GLAZES
OF PINK, BLUE, GREEN, ORANGE AND BROWN. STOKE-ON-TRENT
(MINTON FACTORY) ABOUT 1860. HEIGHT, $8\frac{3}{4}$ IN.
82B. FIGURE, CANEWARE, DECORATED IN 'MAJOLICA' GLAZES
OF MAUVE, WHITE, GREEN AND YELLOW. STOKE-ON-TRENT
MINTON. DATE MARK FOR 1861 LENGTH, 7 IN.
See page 39

83. DISH, EARTHENWARE, DECORATED WITH 'MAJOLICA' GLAZES
OF LIGHT AND DARK GREEN, BROWN, BLUE, YELLOW AND RED
STOKE-ON-TRENT. MINTON. DATE MARK FOR 1871
HEIGHT, $19\frac{1}{4}$ IN.
See page 39

84A. VASE, PORCELAIN, WITH HAND PIERCED DECORATION BY
WILLIAM OWEN. WORCESTER; ABOUT 1895. HEIGHT, $5\frac{1}{4}$ IN.
See pages 39, 40

84B. FLOWER VASE, PORCELAIN, WITH RAISED FLOWER SPRAYS
ON A GRAY GROUND BETWEEN BANDS OF DARK BLUE GROUND
STOKE-ON-TRENT. MINTON; ABOUT 1885. HEIGHT, $6\frac{3}{4}$ IN.
See page 39

85A. PLAQUE, PORCELAIN, PAINTED IN WHITE SLIP BY T. J.
BOTT. WORCESTER; ABOUT 1885. HEIGHT, 11 IN.
85B. INKSTAND, PORCELAIN, STAINED BLACK AND DECORATED IN
WHITE PÂTE SUR PÂTE BY M.L. SOLON AND GILT. MARK
'MINTONS' IMPRESSED, DATE MARK FOR 1890. HEIGHT, 5 IN.

See page 41

86. VASE, EARTHENWARE, DECORATED IN WHITE, BLUE AND
BROWN SLIPS AND PAINTED IN RAISED GOLD. MARK 'DOULTON &
RIX'S PATENT MARQUETERIE 12.7.1887'
HEIGHT, $8\frac{3}{4}$ IN.
See page 37

87. VASE, PORCELAIN, WITH PIERCED DECORATION ON A BROWN
GROUND AND GILDING. MARK 'BROWNFIELD' IMPRESSED
COBRIDGE ('BROWNFIELD & SON'S FACTORY)
ABOUT 1890
HEIGHT, 10¾ IN.
See page 37

88. JUG, BUFF STONEWARE, DECORATED WITH INCISED
DRAWINGS BY HANNAH BARLOW AND WITH BROWN AND BLUE
GLAZES. MARK 'DOULTON LAMBETH 1876 HB. WB'
HEIGHT, $9\frac{1}{4}$ IN.
See page 42

89. VASE, BUFF STONEWARE, WITH A BROWN GROUND PAINTED
IN LIGHT BROWN AND ORANGE SLIPS. MARK 'R W MARTIN &
BROS SOUTHALL 7 1887'
HEIGHT, $9\frac{1}{4}$ IN.
See page 42

90. JUG, STONEWARE, DECORATED IN BLUE, WHITE, YELLOW
AND BROWN SLIPS. MARK 'MARTIN BROS. LONDON & SOUTHALL
5. 1900'
HEIGHT, $6\frac{3}{4}$ IN.
Eli Mason Collection
See page 42

91. VASE, STONEWARE, IN THE FORM OF A BIRD WITH
DETACHABLE HEAD. PROBABLY A CARICATURE OF W. E.
GLADSTONE. MARK 'MARTIN BROS. LONDON & SOUTHALL 1900'
HEIGHT, $14\frac{1}{2}$ IN.
Eli Mason Collection
See page 42

92A. JUG OF 'LEOPARD-SKIN' STONEWARE BY H. SIMEON
LAMBETH (DOULTON'S FACTORY); ABOUT 1890. HEIGHT, $7\frac{1}{2}$ IN.
92B. FIGURE GLAZED RED STONEWARE BY LEON SOLON
MARK 'L. SOLON' MINTON; LATE NINETEENTH CENTURY
HEIGHT, $8\frac{1}{2}$ IN.
92C. JUG, OF 'LEOPARD-SKIN' STONEWARE. BY H. SIMEON
LAMBETH (DOULTON'S FACTORY); END OF NINETEENTH CENTURY
HEIGHT, $8\frac{1}{2}$ IN.
J. H. Mott. *See page* 42

93A. VASE, BLUE-GREY AND BLACK STONEWARE. BY F. C. POPE
LAMBETH (DOULTON'S FACTORY); END OF NINETEENTH CENTURY
HEIGHT, 6 IN.

J. H. Mott

93B. VASE, STONEWARE, BY M. V. MARSHALL. LAMBETH
(DOULTON'S FACTORY); END OF NINETEENTH CENTURY
HEIGHT, 8 IN.

J. H. Mott

See page 42

94. VASE, EARTHENWARE, PAINTED IN LUSTRE ON A BLUE
GROUND. MARK 'W DE MORGAN & CO SANDS END POTTERY'
FULHAM; 1888–98
Victoria and Albert Museum
See page 41

95. DISH, EARTHENWARE, DECORATED IN RED AND YELLOW
LUSTRE. FULHAM (WILLIAM DE MORGAN'S FACTORY)
ABOUT 1880
DIAM. 14 IN.
See page 41

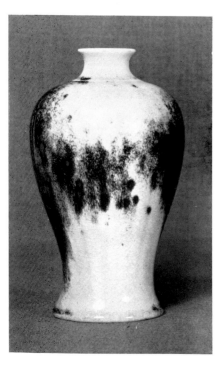

96A. BOWL, PORCELAIN, WITH A LUSTROUS RED GLAZE
STOKE-ON-TRENT (BERNARD MOORE); LATE NINETEENTH
CENTURY. DIAM., 5 IN.

96B. VASE, HARD PASTE PORCELAIN, WITH A DEEP RED FLAMBÉ
GLAZE. STOKE-ON-TRENT (BERNARD MOORE); EARLY TWENTIETH
CENTURY. MARK 'BERNARD MO' IN BLUE. HEIGHT, $7\frac{3}{4}$ IN.

96C. VASE, EARTHENWARE, WITH A DEEP RED GLAZE. MARK
'RUSKIN POTTERY WEST SMETHWICK' IMPRESSED; LATE
NINETEENTH CENTURY. HEIGHT, 7 IN.

See pages 42, 43

T